Sacred Soul Spaces: Designing Your Personal Oasis

A Hands-on Manual for Designing Your Home and Office

Lisa Poundstone, PhD

Certified Advanced Past Life Regression Coach,
Accredited Staging Professional

Published in Olympia, WA, USA

Cover & page design by: Sheena Marie Hamilton, Natural Lynx LLC
Front cover picture by: Sheena Marie Hamilton, Natural Lynx LLC
Home interior pictures by: Lisa Poundstone
Author portrait by: Ben Leavitt

ISBN: 978-1-7324088-0-7

www.SacredSoulDesign.com

Contents

Preface

This hands-on manual is a culmination of my life's work, both personal and professional. I feel as though I have had several lifetimes of adventures and experiences in this one human incarnation, and I know there are many more to come.

I was born to a mother who was interested in esoteric/metaphysical spirituality, so my spiritual awareness began early in life. My mother took astrology classes at night when I was a young girl, and I would sit in the classroom quietly drawing animals, taking in the astrological information unconsciously. She had a circle of friends that consisted of other astrologers, tarot card readers, psychics and witches. We would often visit the esoteric spiritual store near our home, where they sold books, incense, jewelry, stones, crystals, essential oils and other spiritual tools and gifts. This was my normal life.

At the age of thirteen, my mother moved me to Yelm, Washington to attend classes and events at the Ramtha School of Enlightenment. Ramtha is an ascended entity that is channeled through JZ Knight. At first I was angry with my mother for moving me away from my friends, but after a year or so, I settled in and joined her at the Ramtha events. I learned, in those early days, that we create our reality, through energy and consciousness (and sometimes unconsciousness). We can manifest our dreams and desires. I learned that we are One with the Universal Source, that we are not separate. I also learned that people, animals and experiences that come into our lives are there to teach us wisdom we haven't gained yet, as well as to provide information from the Universe. Ramtha called these "Runners." Our job was to gain wisdom from a situation so as not to have to repeat it, then move on to the next learning experience.

At the age of sixteen, I decided I did not want to attend any more classes at the Ramtha School. I felt I had learned what I needed. Instead, I focused my energy on school, my job, dancing and

Preface

science. I had decided at the age of nine that I wanted to study sharks when I grew up because I had read a book about Eugenie Clark, the shark lady. Sharks and other marine animals, particularly dolphins and whales, fascinated me and I wanted to learn all about them. I decided to get a degree in Marine Biology in college and started down that path.

After high school, I went straight to college at The Evergreen State College in Olympia, Washington, near my home in Yelm. Evergreen is a very different type of college in that there were no grades given, only written evaluations. The classes were not traditional either. Instead of taking individual classes that had nothing to do with each other, we took "programs" that revolved around a central concept. We would learn different methods of examining that concept by way of different subjects, allowing us to see the topic in a more holistic, big picture way. One of my high school teachers had encouraged me to do something different than a science program my first year at Evergreen because the final three years would be nothing but science. In my first year, I took a program called, "Through African Arts: Africa and Her Diaspora." In that yearlong program, we learned about African music, dance, literature, film, politics and sociology. It helped to plant a seed in my head for my future directions.

For the remainder of college, I took science-based courses that would help me achieve my goal of attaining a career in Marine Biology studying sharks. After college, I went straight into graduate school at the University of Chicago, where I had a joint position at the Field Museum of Natural History. I earned my PhD in Organismal Biology and Anatomy, specifically studying the batoid fishes, which are flat sharks including stingrays, skates, guitarfish, manta rays and all of their relatives.

After completing a yearlong postdoctoral position at the Field Museum, I got a tenure-track professor position at a small private liberal arts college in Ohio. I taught Zoology for non-majors as well as Animal Physiology and Comparative Anatomy to pre-med majors. The summer before moving to Ohio, I also taught Marine Vertebrate Biology at a Marine Lab in Maine. Although I loved learning about the animals, I decided that teaching college students was not my best outlet. I had chosen to not go the "publish or parish" research route for my career, so I needed to find a new direction for my life.

During my post-doc, I had been reintroduced to the Ramtha School on a visit back home at Christmas time. The information being taught in the school at that time was very science heavy, which excited me greatly. They were learning about brain physiology, molecules of emotion and quantum mechanics and how science is able to explain the spiritual things we were learning. I decided to get involved with the teachings again at that point.

I moved back home to Washington State after leaving academics and ended up meeting my first husband at a Ramtha event. Because I was in a career transition, I chose to learn the business he was in, which was mortgage. We started a mortgage reduction education company together, so I read a lot of books on business and marketing quickly to get myself up to speed on how to run a business. Fast-forward five years, and we were divorcing each other and the business. I wanted out of the industry to be as far away from him as possible, so it was time to figure out my next move. I also left the Ramtha School for a second time, but continued my spiritual learning in other arenas.

I decided to follow my artistic passion and started a home staging and interior design business. I trained directly with the creator of the home staging concept, Barb Schwarz; I took a feng shui course with a Chinese feng shui master; and I read numerous books on design and space planning. I am now in my tenth year in the design industry and have had the opportunity to design and stage several thousand homes.

In June of 2017, I decided to take my spiritual life to a new level. I trained under the direction of world-renowned spiritual teacher and author, Denise Linn, and became a certified Advanced Past

Life Regression coach. Since then, I've been working with clients to help them release blockages and limitations in their lives, as well as access their hidden talents and abilities. I've been connecting them with their deceased loves ones and spiritual messengers and guides. In working with my clients in the spiritual realm, I have deepened my spiritual awareness and opened up my intuition to a new level of consciousness. I notice universal signs and messages daily.

When the outside world is filled with chaos and confusion, I am able to retreat to my own personal Sacred Soul Space within my home. I am surrounded by inspiration and possibility, and I am comforted and grounded. I have created my sanctuary. This manual was written in this special sanctuary, providing inspiration for me to share my vast wisdom and experience with you. As a culmination of my knowledge, I have combined science, color theory, space planning, feng shui and spirituality to create Sacred Soul Space Design. I break down the design process into simple, actionable steps, so you can follow along and know what to do in your own space. I want to help you to design your own Sacred Soul Space.

Acknowledgments

This book could not have been written without the help and support of my friends, family and teachers.

I want to thank Denise Linn, who certified me as an Advanced Past Life Regression Coach. Her wisdom inspires me daily.

I am thankful for my coach and mentor, Morgana Rae, for her guidance and support in writing this book.

I am grateful for my life partner, Skip Thompson, and my two children, Nohwa and Curran, for supporting me in writing this manual and loving me through it. I am grateful to my mother, Sharon Rosenberger, for introducing me to the spiritual journey I have been on in this life.

I am thankful for my amazing friend, Whitney Kershner, who helped inspire me to write the content of this book. I am also thankful for my friend and designer, Jennifer Hay, for her daily help in beautifying our clients' homes.

I am especially thankful for Alison Bailey, who helped me to edit and put this manual together for publication, as well as Sheena Hamilton for designing the cover and interior of the manual.

"Environment is stronger than willpower."

Buckminster Fuller

1

Introduction to Sacred Soul Space Design

What is a Sacred Soul Space?

We are often bombarded in our busy, chaotic lives. Wrapped up in technology, we are pulled away from who we truly are. We clutter our homes and offices, which then clutters our minds.

Designing a Sacred Soul Space in your home or office will give you a place to escape, a peaceful oasis, to re-center yourself and remember who you truly are and what you can create.

A Sacred Soul Space is a room or home that is tailored to the person it is designed for, based on their desires and goals. It can be a peaceful, healing room for meditation, yoga and other spiritual practices. It can also be an inspiring, expansive space for helping to fulfill life goals and dreams. It can be a combination of these ideas, so long as the intentions don't conflict with each other.

Color is an important part of the Sacred Soul Space design concept, as each color has a different effect on people at the psychological and physiological level. Although you may like a particular set of colors, they may not be the best ones to use in a Sacred Soul Space design if they have the opposite effect of what you are trying to achieve.

Feng shui plays a key role in designing a Sacred Soul Space, as the amount of furniture, artwork and accessories present greatly affect how a room feels and how the energy flows.

To achieve a true Sacred Soul Space, the feeling and look of the room have to be in alignment with the person it is designed for. It has to be clear of old and negative energy, as well as clear of clutter and chaos. It needs to include items that have special meaning to you or to the intent of the space itself. The key is that the space incorporates specific intentions with the greatest possible outcome in mind.

My years of study and training in a wide range of spiritual practices have helped me hone my intuition and knowingness about what a space needs to be in harmony and unity with the person for whom it is designed. Each space has its own distinct feeling and beauty, just as each individual person is unique in their own right.

Personal taste and style have everything to do with making a room truly unique and inspiring to the person who resides in it most. You may end up modifying your assumptions about how you want to design a room for your own personal oasis based on what you learn as we go through the steps of the design process. You will learn about the scientific meanings and effects of colors and scents, as well as balance and space planning of furnishings for energy flow and comfort. I encourage you to be as open to the process as possible to allow new ideas to flow in. Don't be afraid to try things out, and if they don't work for you, try something different.

Home Furnishing Initial Assessment – Taste and Preference

Before you begin to design your Sacred Soul Space, it is important to get in touch with what you are trying to create. Not only is it important that your space is aesthetically pleasing to your eyes, but it must also provide feelings and smells that will nourish your soul, stimulate your imagination or provide comfort and relaxation – whatever it is you are trying to achieve in your Sacred Soul Space.

After going through the steps in this manual to design one room in your home or office, you may choose to focus on additional rooms that activate different desires you want to support. My recommendation is to focus on only one space at a time, so that the room truly reflects your intentions for it and the process doesn't get confusing or overwhelming.

The following questions will help you establish a starting point in your design process. Please note that although you may be drawn to certain things at the beginning of these steps, you may decide that a new direction is warranted once you are presented with the detailed information in this manual. Don't be ashamed to start again.

Think about your current home, and answer the following questions.

- What is your favorite room in your home? Why?

  _____

  _____

- Which pieces of furniture do you love?

  _____

  _____

- Which pieces of furniture do you really not like?

  _____

  _____

- Which pieces of art do you love?

  _____

  _____

- Which pieces of art could you do without?

  _____

  _____

- What are your favorite décor pieces?

  _____

  _____

- What drew you to them?

  _____

  _____

INTRODUCTION
TO SACRED SOUL
SPACE DESIGN

- Do you have décor you really dislike? Which pieces?

  _____

  _____

- Which colors do you have in your home?

  _____

  _____

- Do you like your colors?

  _____

  _____

- How do your colors make you feel?

  _____

  _____

- Do you have any rugs or floor coverings that you love?

  _____

  _____

Think about furniture and home furnishings in general, and answer the following questions.

- Do you have one particular style of furniture that you love? What is it?

  _____

  _____

- Do you have multiple styles that speak to you? What are they?

  _____

  _____

- Are you drawn to any particular era of time for furniture?

  _____

  _____

- Are you drawn to particular geographical regions for furnishing styles?

  _____

  _____

Think about symbols, other cultures and animals, and answer the following questions.

- Are there any symbols that speak to you from other cultures?

  _____

  _____

- Are there particular cultures you are really drawn to in general?

  _____

  _____

- What animals do you love or admire?

  _____

  _____

- If you were any kind of animal, what kind would you be?

  _____

  _____

- Do you have any collections of particular animals in your home or office?

  _____

  _____

Think about geographical locations around the world, different climates and scents and aromas, and answer the following questions.

- Which countries have you visited that you love?

  _____

  _____

- Which countries do you really want to visit?

  _____

  _____

- What is your favorite type of terrain to be in (i.e., beach, woods or forest, rain forest, desert, meadow, canyon, cave, rolling hills, etc.)?

  _____

  _____

- What is your favorite climate to be in (i.e., tropical, cold-weather, temperate, arid, etc.)?

  _____

  _____

- Which scents and aromas do you love?

  _____

  _____

- Are there any scents from nature you are drawn to?

  _____

  _____

Begin the Journey to Create Your Space

Now that you have answered these questions, your mind is beginning to open up to your desires and inspirations. Take yourself on a journey within your initial Sacred Space. You may want to record yourself speaking in order to play it back, so that you can be truly immersed in your journey.

Find a comfortable, relaxed position. Close your eyes and take several deep breaths, allowing your mind and body to relax. Melt into the surface below you. Allow yourself to go deeper and deeper into your subconscious mind. You are safe. You are secure. All is well. Become one with your breath. Become one with your surroundings.

Now that you are relaxed, in your mind's eye, transport yourself to a place where you feel safe and secure. This can be a place you've been before or one that exists in your imagination. It can be inside or outside. Notice your surroundings. Where are you? What images do you see? What sounds do you hear? What scents do you smell? Are you alone or are there people or animals around you? Take some moments to fully be present in your surroundings. (Pause)

You will now find a place to sit down. This could be a chair or it could be the ground or something else. Go ahead and sit down and get comfortable. As you are sitting down, comfortable, taking in your surroundings, you notice a mist start to form in the distance. The mist becomes thicker and thicker as it starts rolling towards you. You know this mist is safe. The mist comes closer and closer to you and finally surrounds you where you cannot see anything - you can only feel that you are safe and secure within the mist.

As the mist is twirling around you, a door appears in the distance. You walk towards the door, knowing that on the other side of the door is your very own Sacred Soul Space. You open the door and step inside, looking down at your feet.

As you slowly lift your head, you are able to see what kind of room you are in. What colors do you see? What kind of furniture is in the room? Notice any particular pieces of artwork that stand out. Take a look at the details of the accessories. What type of fabrics and soft surfaces are in the room? How do you feel being there? Pay attention to any particular smells that are wafting through the air. Take some time to walk around this room, noticing the fine details. (Pause)

When you feel like you have noticed the details of the space, leave the room and come back to the here and now.

Take a few moments to write down thoughts about what you saw in the space. Try to be as detailed as you can, so that you can refer back to this when designing your Sacred Soul Space. Write down the colors you noticed and where they were throughout the room. What kind of furniture did you see? What was special about it? What artwork and décor were present in the room?

_____

_____

_____

_____

_____

_____

_____

_____

_____

_____

_____

_____

Now it's time to leap into the nitty-gritty elements of designing your own Sacred Soul Space.

2

Clearing Your Space

Before you can begin to design your Sacred Soul Space, it is important to remove all clutter. What is clutter? Clutter can be paperwork or receipts, artwork and photos, accessories and collections, furniture, clothing and shoes, junk, and other similar items. I also recommend that you clear the existing energy by using the smudging process describe below. This will give you a fresh, clean slate on which to design your beautiful Sacred Soul Space.

Why Clutter Clearing Works

There are numerous scientific studies on how clutter affects us psychologically as well as physiologically. Some of the psychological issues clutter can cause include low subjective well being, unhealthier eating, poorer mental health, less efficient visual processing and less efficient thinking (Psychology Today).

In physiological terms, clutter in a space creates chaos in the mind. It can create breathing problems, mental confusion and overall discomfort. It also stifles the energy flowing through a room, so that the energy is stagnant and feels heavy and oppressive or claustrophobic.

Clutter can drain your energy both mentally and physically. It causes stress, anxiety and tension. It can make it harder to get a good night's sleep. It can take away time because you are unable to find things easily. It can also cause you to spend more money than you would otherwise because you don't know what you have in your home already.

On a visual level, clutter takes away the beauty of your home. When you have too much stuff, it is hard to see some of the beautiful features your home might possess. It can take away from an amazing view. It can distract from beautiful and meaningful pieces of art and décor.

When a room is clutter free, it feels open and expansive. There is room to move around. It creates possibility and uplifts the spirit. It is calming. You will be more productive in your time. You may shed excess pounds without trying. It will help you to release the past emotionally. It will help you to have more focused mental clarity. It can remove blockages in creativity. It will help with allergies due to less surface area for dust to collect. It opens you up to opportunity. It can give you more energy and bring happiness to your space.

Smudging to Clear Energy

What is smudging? It is a process using the smoke from dried herbs to cleanse and clear the air and energy from a space to renew and refresh it. Native Americans and other indigenous peoples have used smudging as a cleansing and clearing ritual since ancient times. Although some view it as a "new age" thing, there is actually modern science to back up its benefits (Mohagheghzadeh, Faridi, Shams-Ardakani, Ghasemi, 2006).

Scientific Benefits

There are numerous scientific benefits to smudging your space. It cleanses the air of unwanted bacteria. In fact, scientific studies have found that up to 94% of bacteria is killed off for up to 24 hours after smudging. It clears the air of dust, pet dander, mold spores, pollen and other allergens. It produces negative ions, which increases overall well-being, improves mental focus and memory and increases energy, so it can be used as a natural anti-depressant. It also improves sleep patterns by regulating serotonin levels. It calms and relaxes the body, relieving stress and tension.

Spiritual Benefits

Indigenous people and those who are spiritually inclined use smudging for other ethereal purposes. Smudging can clear negative energy from emotions held in a room, including anger, anxiety, fear, depression and grief. It can cleanse objects that hold negative energy from previous owners. It increases clarity and awareness, heightens wisdom and quickens the senses.

Personally I have used smudging to clear my home of negative energy after certain people have visited, as well as to rid it of ghosts and spirits my kids and I have experienced in our homes.

Smudging can be done with different herbs including sage, cedar and sweetgrass, among others, depending on your desires. Sage is used for healing, as well as to bless, cleanse and heal a person, object or house. White sage is for purifying and clearing negative energy. Black sage is for protection. Cedar is used for protection and cleansing. Sweetgrass is used for blessing and reminding us of the feminine essence of the Earth. You may have a local shop that sells smudging herbs, or you can purchase them online.

Smudging process

Smudging can be as practical or as spiritual a process as you want to make it for yourself and your Sacred Soul Space. As a spiritual practice, the most important thing is to hold your intent for what the smoke is doing to clear your space of negative energy. You may choose to do incantations as you clear each room, or you can hold the thought in your head.

It's a good idea to open up a window to ventilate your space as you are going through the process. To begin, light your smudge herbs with a lighter or matches. Gently blow out the flame to create a smoldering effect with smoke coming off of the herbs, like you would with an incense stick. You may need to relight the herb a few times during the process to keep the smoke going. Place the herb in a fire safe bowl or abalone shell to keep the ashes from getting all over your space as you move around the room.

Before you move around the room or house, smudge yourself first. You can use your hand or a feather to help direct the smoke over your body. Start at your feet and move up to your head and then back down to your feet to complete the process, circling your body.

Once you have smudged yourself, you are ready to smudge your Sacred Space. Begin at the door and then move clockwise around the room, wafting smoke into every corner and edge of the room, as energy tends to be most stagnant in the corners. Because smoke rises, start low and move upwards in the corners. Get inside closets and cabinets if applicable. Once you have done the outer edges, stand in the center of the room. While you are waving the smoke around the room to fill it up, hold the image of the smoke clearing away negative energy in your head. Your intent is very powerful in this process.

If you are smudging more than just one room, continue moving in a clockwise direction to the next room and repeat the process. Continue to smudge each space thoroughly until the entire house has been cleared.

When you have completed the process, snuff out the herb by grinding it into the bowl, dipping it into sand or letting it burn out on its own.

Smudging

🍃 Remove everything from the room you are designing, if possible. If it isn't possible to remove everything, take out anything that isn't a large piece of furniture.

🍃 Once items have been cleared from the room, take the time to smudge the space to clear out old, stagnant and negative energy.

3

Understanding the
Science of Color

Before you decide which colors you are going to introduce to your Sacred Soul Space, it is important to know what each color represents and what it can do to you psychologically and physiologically. Each color vibrates at a different frequency and holds its own unique energy.

Choosing colors for your sacred space will depend on what your desired intentions are for the room. Have you ever wondered why some interiors of homes and businesses appeal to you, while others don't? Have you noticed that certain types of businesses use similar colors in their branding and physical appearance? Colors affect us psychologically and physiologically at the subconscious level. Each color stimulates different parts of our mind and can elicit both positive and negative feelings.

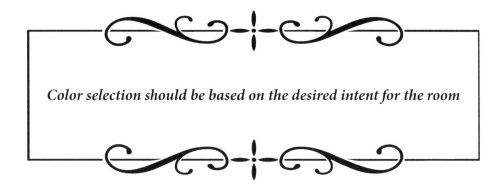

Color selection should be based on the desired intent for the room

Before we delve into the meanings of the colors, I want you to take a journey into the colors to truly experience the energy and frequency they possess. You might want to record yourself reading aloud through the journey, so that you can play it back and re-live the experience of the journey as if you were having it first-hand.

Alternatively, you could ask a trusted friend or family member to take you on the following journey. I have done this journey in my workshop and attendees were amazed at how each color truly did feel different to them. This exercise fosters the opportunity to have an experience with each color rather than just absorbing the intellectual meanings that you have to trust are true.

A Journey Through the Colors

Each color has its own special meaning and resonates at its own unique frequency. Each one affects us on a psychological and physiological level. I want you now to fully immerse yourself into the colors to feel their energy and power. As you are doing this journey of the colors, take note in your mind as to how each one makes you feel. What images come to mind for each color? You may want to record yourself talking through the journey so you can play it back to fully immerse yourself in the colors.

Sit or lie down in a comfortable position, relaxing your body. Take slow, deep breaths, allowing your mind to release all thoughts. Allow your body to relax, letting go of all tension. As you continue breathing slowly and deeply, your relaxation becomes deeper and deeper. Take time to relax your body and your mind.

Now that you are relaxed, imagine a colorful rainbow in front of you. It is a beautiful rainbow with the most glorious colors, shining like bright lights, shimmering, pulsating. Each color blends into the next, and yet each holds its own separate space as well. Walk towards the rainbow until you reach the very edge.

Jump into the red of the rainbow. See the color red all around you. Feel the energy red possesses. How does it make your body feel? What thoughts does it bring up in your mind? Notice any positive or negative emotions or images that come up for you. Hold the image of red in your mind. See it. Feel it.

Now you will gently float through the color red towards orange, noticing how the colors merge and change. Stop yourself when glowing orange light surrounds you. Look at the orange. Feel the orange. How does it make you feel? What images come to mind as you are surrounded by orange?

Float out of the orange into the yellow light. Surround yourself in yellow. How does yellow make you feel? What images do you see in the yellow? Are there any emotions that come up as you sit within the yellow? Feel the frequency of yellow.

From the yellow, gently float towards green, surrounding yourself in glowing green light. Feel the energy of green. How do you feel? What do you see? Fully immerse yourself in green. What images and emotions come up when you are in green?

Transition now from green to turquoise/teal on your way to blue. Take a pause in the teal, a mixture of green and blue. Notice how teal has different energy than green. Notice how teal makes you feel. Notice images that come up as you sit in the teal glowing light.

Continue floating towards the blue and stop when you are fully surrounded by glowing blue light. Feel the frequency of blue. Immerse yourself in blue. What emotions come up for you? What images do you see? How does blue make you feel?

Float now towards purple and stop when you are fully immersed in glowing purple light. Look at the purple all around you. Notice how you feel when surrounded by purple. Notice the images that come to you in purple light. Be the purple.

Continue floating into magenta as you circle back around near the red. Surround yourself with the glowing magenta light. How does magenta make you feel? What do you see when you are in the middle of magenta?

Now, while you are inside of magenta, see a bright white light in front of you. Imagine that the white light is softening the magenta to form a lighter pink color. Surround yourself with this light pink glowing energy. How do you feel inside of pink? What images come up with pink?

Float towards the center of the bright, white light and step into it. The white light surrounds you. How do you feel in the white light? What emotions come up as you are surrounded by white? What images come to you?

In the distance, you now see a spot of total darkness, like a black hole. As you move toward the black, the white is transitioning from light gray to darker gray. Pause for a moment in the gray and fully surround yourself with gray light. Notice how gray makes you feel. Notice the images that come up while you are in gray.

Continue moving toward the black from the gray that is getting darker and darker until you are fully surrounded by thick blackness. As you sit in the black, how do you feel? What positive or negative emotions come up for you? What images do you see in the black?

As you are surrounded by black, you notice that the black is beginning to lighten and the color is changing around you. The color is turning brown. You are now in brown energy, brown frequency. Feel the brown. See the brown. What images come to you as you are enveloped by brown? What emotions come up in the brown?

As you are in the middle of brown, notice a shimmering gold light in the distance. Jump out of the brown and into the gold to fully immerse yourself in golden light. Notice the energy of gold. How do you feel and what images do you see?

The gold now starts to transition to a luminous, silver light. Surround yourself in silver. Pay attention to how you feel inside of silver. What images do you notice in silver?

Gently come back to the present time and space. Open your eyes.

UNDERSTANDING
THE SCIENCE OF
COLOR

Make notes below on each of the colors and how you felt being surrounded by them. Were the emotions positive or negative or something else? What images did you see? What colors did you love? Were there any that you strongly disliked?

Red makes me feel:

_____

_____

Red images that come to mind:

_____

_____

Orange makes me feel:

_____

_____

Orange images that come to mind:

_____

_____

Yellow makes me feel:

_____

_____

Yellow images that come to mind:

_____

_____

Green makes me feel:

_____

_____

Green images that come to mind:

_____

_____

Turquoise/Teal makes me feel:

_____

_____

Turquoise/Teal images that come to mind:

_____

_____

Blue makes me feel:

_____

_____

Blue images that come to mind:

_____

_____

Purple makes me feel:

_____

_____

Purple images that come to mind:

_____

_____

Magenta makes me feel:

_____

_____

Magenta images that come to mind:

_____

_____

Pink makes me feel:

_____

_____

Pink images that come to mind:

_____

_____

White makes me feel:

_____

_____

White images that come to mind:

_____

_____

Gray makes me feel:

_____

_____

Gray images that come to mind:

_____

_____

Black makes me feel:

_____

_____

Black images that come to mind:

_____

_____

Brown makes me feel:

_____

_____

Brown images that come to mind:

_____

_____

Gold makes me feel:

_____

_____

Gold images that come to mind:

_____

_____

Silver makes me feel:

_____

_____

Silver images that come to mind:

_____

_____

Color Theory – Meanings and Uses

Colors are generally grouped into a few major categories: warm, cool, neutral and transitional. Energetic, stimulating, warm colors include red, yellow and orange. Blues, greens and purples are cool, soothing and relaxing. There are colors that transition between warm and cool tones, as all colors reside on a spectral continuum.

Although colors including brown, black, white, gray, gold and silver are classified as neutral colors, they still affect us in ways that need to be understood before using them. Their neutrality relates to how they pair with other colors rather than the underlying psychological and physiological responses they trigger.

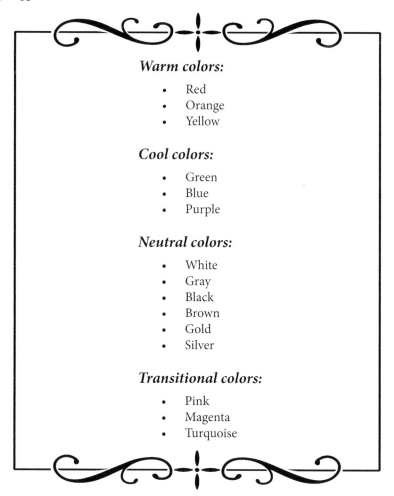

Warm colors:

- Red
- Orange
- Yellow

Cool colors:

- Green
- Blue
- Purple

Neutral colors:

- White
- Gray
- Black
- Brown
- Gold
- Silver

Transitional colors:

- Pink
- Magenta
- Turquoise

Now that you have immersed yourself into each of the colors addressed in this manual, see how closely your experiences, feelings and images are to the explanations of the colors below. Because I have included a section in this manual on crystals/stones, I have made note of stones that fall into each color for cross-reference.

See Appendix 2 on page 133 for a list of common stones/crystals sorted by both color and name.

Red: Energy and passion

Do you want to create energy and passion in your home?

Red is a highly energetic color that excites emotions and can motivate action. It can give confidence where it is lacking, and can promote ambition and determination. It is the color of physical movement. As the color of sexuality, it can also stimulate deeper and more intense passions within us.

Because it is such a strong color, red triggers strong emotions and has associations including love, lust, heat, strength, leadership, willpower, danger, rage, and anger. It also represents power and courage.

Physiologically, red is known to elevate blood pressure, increase respiratory rates, increase metabolism, enhance libido, elevate levels of energy, and increase confidence and enthusiasm.

Red is a great color to use in high-energy rooms, as it is an appetite and conversation stimulant. There is a really good reason why a lot of successful restaurants have red in their branding and interior décor. Red is best used in moderation as an accent color in living rooms, dining rooms and kitchens.

If you want to create passion in the bedroom, you can use red, but beware of using too much, as it can create hatred and agitation. A little pop of red in a bedroom can go a long way. Green is a great color to use to counteract the effects of too much red in a room.

In our country, people who want to exude power wear red (think red power tie). In other cultures, however, red actually represents purity, joy, good luck and prosperity. My recommendation is to use it how you see fit, keeping in mind that it may produce enhanced emotions. Pay attention to how you feel around red.

- Highly energetic
- Passion
- Power
- Confidence

- Sexuality
- Appetite stimulant
- Good accent for living rooms, dining rooms and kitchens

Red Stones: *Cinnabar, Coral, Garnet, Jasper, Ruby, Tourmaline*

Orange: Warm and comforting

Do you want to have joy, inspiration and expansion in your life?

Orange is a mixture of red and yellow, with all the warmth and comfort of those colors, creating happiness and optimism. It is the color of adventure and social communication. It uplifts us in a way other colors do not.

Orange relates to our "gut instincts," as opposed to the physical reaction of red and the mental stimulation of yellow. It aids in the assimilation of new ideas and frees the spirit of limitations. It gives us the freedom to be ourselves. It helps us overcome grief and bounce back from disappointments. It also inspires a positive outlook on life and keeps us motivated and looking on the bright side.

Orange encourages breaking out of the box and tapping into adventure and risk-taking. It inspires physical confidence, competition and independence.

Some oranges, such as the color of pumpkins and fall leaves, are appetite and conversation stimulants and good for use in the dining room and kitchen. Orange also helps with creativity, imagination and expansion, so it can be used in an office and craft room. Although it does not have the negative affects of red and yellow, it is probably the most under-used color of our time.

I personally love orange in home furnishings, as it adds friendly warmth that red and yellow are missing. I love combining it with teal and lime green in my own home.

It is not a coincidence that orange essential oil is known to carry the energy and frequency of the color in it, creating some of the emotions mentioned above. Orange oil helps with anxiety, calming, uplifting, and bringing in abundance. It has a sense of humor and is playful, as well as generous, spontaneous, creative and joyful.

- Inspiration
- Expansion
- Optimism
- Social communication
- Uplifting
- Motivating

- Independence
- Creativity
- Appetite stimulant
- Good for dining rooms, kitchens, offices and craft rooms

Orange Stones: *Agate, Calcite, Carnelian, Creedite, Quartz, Salt Lamp, Selenite, Soapstone*

Yellow: Cheery and invigorating

Do you want to create a happy, uplifting environment?

The right shade of yellow can help with this. It can offer hope, fun and cheerfulness. It also creates enthusiasm for life and can generate optimism and confidence.

Yellow is the color of the mind and intellect. It resonates with the left, logical side of the brain, stimulating mental abilities and creating mental perception and agility. It inspires original thought and inquisitiveness. Although it helps to inspire new ideas and new ways of doing things, it is from the practical side rather than the dreaming, right side of the brain. It helps with making decisions as related to clarity of thought and ideas. It can help us focus and recall information as well (think about legal yellow paper pads).

On the downside, yellow can create anxiety and agitation because it is a fast moving color. It can also make someone more mentally analytical and critical. It is the most difficult color for the eye to take in, and it can be overpowering if overused. Yellow, like red, has a negative effect on some people, making it easier to lose your temper and cause upset in babies.

Yellow enhances concentration and speeds metabolism, making it a good color for kitchen and dining areas, as well as offices.

Yellow accents are easier to add into a room than picking the perfect yellow paint. If you do want to paint a room with the color, my recommendation is to stay with a yellow that is closer to a soft butter color rather than an intensely bright sun yellow.

- Happy
- Hopeful
- Cheerful
- Confidence
- Optimism
- Intellect

- Inspiring
- Clarity
- Focus and Concentration
- Good for dining rooms, kitchens and offices

Yellow Stones: *Amber, Chrysoprase, Citrine, Danburite, Desert Rose, Diamond, Garnet, Golden Healer Lemurians, Honey Dogtooth Calcite, Jasper, Kunzite, Moonstone, Onyx, Pyrite, Sapphire, Soapstone, Tiger's Eye, Topaz, Tourmaline*

Green: Refresh, renew and restore

Do you want to renew your health, increase your wealth and get in touch with nature?

Green is a mixture of blue and yellow, so it can be a calming color that refreshes. It inspires hope and a generosity of spirit from its blue side. It renews and restores depleted energy and activates mental clarity and optimism from its yellow side. It is the color of balance, harmony and growth.

Green symbolizes nature and the outdoors, so using it in your home can bring the outside indoors. It is the color of those that love the garden, the home and hosting friends and family. It is an emotionally positive color, which gives us the ability to love and nurture others and ourselves unconditionally.

Green is also the color of health, and balances the heart and the emotions. As a color of growth, it represents spring, renewal and rebirth. It restores depleted energy and restores a sense of well-being.

Green represents prosperity and abundance of financial and material wealth. It is great for the business world, real estate and property. On the negative side, it can also be possessive and materialistic, so that is something to watch out for.

Green is the easiest color on the eye and can improve vision. Green can be used in most rooms of the house without any negative effect. It pairs well with most if not all other colors, so it is easy to add to homes and offices.

- Renewal
- Balance
- Harmony
- Growth
- Health

- Energy
- Prosperity
- Abundance
- Good for any room in the house

Green Stones: Agate, Apatite, Apophyllite, Aquamarine, Aventurine, Chrysoprase, Dioptase, Emerald, Fluorite, Green Kyanite, Halite, Jade, Jasper, Kunzite, Malachite, Moldavite, Onyx, Peridot, Prehnite, Quartz, Sapphire, Serpentine, Soapstone, Tourmaline, Turquoise

Teal/Turquoise: Open communication and clarity of thought

Do you want to have open communication, clarity of thought and heightened intuition?

Teal, interchangeable for turquoise, is a friendly, happy color that opens communication between the heart and spoken word. As a combination of blue with a bit of yellow (and green), it has the calm tranquility of blue, the growth and balance of green and the uplifting energy of yellow. It controls and heals the emotions by creating emotional balance and stability.

Teal aids concentration and clarity of thought, calming the nervous system. It gives control over self-expression and builds confidence. It helps in decision-making, including in emergency situations.

Teal enhances empathy and caring and can encourage inner healing. It recharges the spirit in times of mental stress and can alleviate feelings of loneliness. It heightens creativity and sensitivity, as well as intuitive ability and spiritual growth. It helps to build self-esteem and self-love.

Too much teal may lead to an overactive mind and create emotional imbalance. Too little may cause a withholding of emotions.

Teal is a good color to use in living rooms, bedrooms, bathrooms and offices. It can be used in a minimal way in dining rooms and kitchens if it is closer to the green side to give it more energy, or if it is paired with high energy colors like red, orange and yellow.

- Open communication
- Emotional balance
- Clarity
- Confidence
- Decision making
- Empathy

- Intuition
- Self-esteem
- Self-love
- Good for most rooms in the house

Teal/Turquoise Stones: *Amazonite, Aquamarine, Chrysocolla, Opal, Selenite, Turquoise*

Blue: Calm and relaxing

Do you want to create a peaceful, calm space and build trust and loyalty?

Blue is the color of trust, honesty, loyalty and responsibility. It promotes both physical and mental relaxation, can reduce stress and creates a sense of calmness, relaxation and order. It slows down the metabolism.

If you are in a business where your clients visit you regularly, having blue walls or blue décor can help promote trust. It helps create inner security and confidence. Studies have shown that people are more productive in blue rooms (Kwallek, Soon, Lewis, 2007).

Blue is a communication color and great for public speaking. It helps us speak the truth and enhances our ability to communicate our needs and wants.

Blue also inspires higher ideals. It has a spiritual aspect to it and enhances contemplation and prayer.

This color is great for bedrooms where people want ease and peace. For a calm, relaxing feeling in the bedroom, you might try a softer blue with or without a hint of green in it. The paler the blue, the more freedom we feel. Darker blues are better for accent pieces rather than for larger walls or furnishings if relaxation is the intent.

Blue is the most universally liked color, so you can't go wrong with using it in most areas of your home and office. I recommend keeping it out of the dining and kitchen if possible, unless you counteract it with a high-energy color. Blue serves as an appetite suppressant, and because it slows down your metabolism, you don't digest your food as quickly in blue rooms.

- Peaceful
- Relaxation
- Trust
- Honesty
- Loyalty
- Freedom

- Confidence
- Communication
- Productive
- Good for living rooms, bedrooms, bathrooms and offices

Blue Stones: Agate, Amazonite, Angelite, Aqua Aura, Aquamarine, Azurite, Quartz, Calcite, Celestine, Chrysocolla, Diamond, Jasper, Kyanite, Lapis Lazuli, Larimar, Moonstone, Onyx, Sapphire, Sodalite, Topaz, Tourmaline, Turquoise

Purple/Violet: Imagination and creativity

Do you want to deepen your spirituality and imagination or feel luxurious?

Purple, which is interchangeable with the term violet, has always been special, representing royalty, spirituality and imagination. It allows us to get in touch with our deeper thoughts and inspires high ideals.

The red side of purple gives energy and strength. The blue side gives spirituality and integrity. This combination creates a balance between our physical and spiritual energies. Violet has the highest vibration or frequency in the visible light spectrum. It expands awareness, connecting us to our higher self or consciousness and assists those who seek spiritual fulfillment. It is associated with the transformation of the soul.

Purple represents the imagination, dreams and the future, while at the same time calming the emotions. It enhances psychic ability and enlightenment while keeping us grounded. It promotes harmony of mind and emotions, and supports the practice of meditation.

Purple inspires unconditional and selfless love. It encourages sensitivity and compassion, although that makes it vulnerable to illness. It is the color of the humanitarian. It is feminine and romantic. It is known for stimulating creativity and originality in artists and dreamers.

Deep purple is powerful and associated with royalty and nobility. It gives the impression of luxury and wealth. It creates ambition and self-assuredness as a leader, demanding respect.

When using purple, one must not overdue it, as large amounts of purple can instill depression and moodiness, particularly in those who are susceptible to depressed states. Adding small pops of purple into your home décor can be a way to bring in the color without overdoing it.

Soft purple tones are great in rooms for meditation and relaxation, whereas deeper purples can make bedrooms and living rooms feel more luxurious.

- Royalty
- Spirituality
- Imagination
- Psychic ability
- Meditation
- Unconditional love
- Sensitivity

- Romantic
- Wealth
- Creativity
- Good for living rooms, bedrooms and spiritual rooms used for meditation and yoga

Purple Stones: *Amethyst, Ametrine, Charoite, Jasper, Kunzite, Lepidolite, Sapphire, Sugilite*

Magenta: Universal harmony and emotional balance

Do you want to create harmony and balance in your life, strengthen your intuition and feel the freedom of your spirit?

Magenta is a combination of red and violet, gaining passion, power and energy from the red side and introspective and quiet energy from the violet side. It is spiritual and practical at the same time, encouraging common sense and a balanced outlook on life.

Magenta helps create harmony and balance on all levels of life including physical, mental, emotional and spiritual. It can strengthen intuition and psychic ability and help you experience greater levels of awareness and knowledge. It helps move things forward and release old emotional patterns, making it a color of change and transformation.

Magenta uplifts the spirits and promotes compassion and kindness. It represents universal love. It creates happiness, contentment, cheerfulness and appreciation for what you have. It generates acceptance, tolerance and patience.

Magenta represents the free spirit, helping to create one's own path. It increases dream activity and helps to turn those dreams into reality. It is innovative and imaginative.

Too much magenta can trigger depression and despair in some people and may not be good for introverts and those with chronic depression. When too much magenta is present, it can create arrogance and bossiness. Green is a good balance color to tone down magenta energy.

You can use magenta in small quantities in the kitchen and dining room due to the energy it receives from the red. It is good in living rooms, bedrooms, and spiritual rooms. Try adding in magenta accents by way of pillows or other home décor.

- Harmony
- Balance
- Psychic ability
- Transformation
- Compassion

- Universal love
- Appreciation
- Free spirit
- Good for living rooms, bedrooms, and spiritual rooms

Magenta Stones: *Cobalto Calcite, Garnet, Ruby, Ruby Fuschite, Sugilite, Watermelon Tourmaline*

Pink: Unconditional love and nurturing

Do you want to foster compassion, unconditional love and nurturing?

Pink is a color of compassion, nurturing and love, related to unconditional love and understanding. As the combination of red and white, it has a need for action, passion and power on the red side and gains insight and openness from the white side. Deeper pinks exhibit more passion and energy.

Pink is a sign of hope, inspiring warm and comforting feelings. It alleviates feelings of anger, aggression, resentment and neglect. It can calm the nerves and create physical weakness, as shown in psychological studies (Gilliam, Unruh, 1988).

Pink is feminine and romantic, thoughtful and caring. It has a gentle loving energy. It helps put people in touch with their nurturing side, whether giving or receiving.

When used too much, pink can be seen as immature and girlish. It can also represent a lack of self-confidence and self-worth. Combining it with darker colors, such as navy, brown, deep purple or black, adds strength and sophistication. Pink pairs well with green, blue and purple. A deeper pink that is close to magenta can be great to combine with orange.

Pink is a good color for bedrooms and spiritual rooms when you want to create love and comfort. If you really like the meaning and effects of pink, but don't want to overdue the color in your space, adding in artwork and décor pieces with pink may fulfill your needs.

- Compassion
- Unconditional love
- Nurturing
- Hope
- Calming

- Romantic
- Caring
- Gentle
- Good for bedrooms and spiritual rooms

Pink Stones: *Calcite, Coral, Danburite, Diamond, Garnet, Halite, Kunzite, Lithium Quartz, Moonstone, Pink Tourmaline, Rhodochrosite, Rhodonite, Rose Quartz, Ruby, Ruby Fuschite, Salt Lamp, Sugilite, Topaz*

White (and Clear): Hope and innocence

Do you want to embody innocence, wholeness and openness?

White is the color of new beginnings, purity and innocence. It is the color of perfection, wholeness and completion. It provides a blank canvas for other colors, similar to brown, and it creates an open path for anything the mind can conceive. It awakens growth, openness and creativity.

White is equality, neutrality and independence. White offers peace and calm, comfort and hope and creates a sense of order and efficiency. It is personified as cleanliness and purity and can help to strengthen your energy system.

On the negative side, too much white can be cold, sterile and uninviting. It can stimulate feelings of emptiness and isolation and create a sense of fear of doing anything because it might be disrupted. It provides little stimulation to the senses, so adding other colors will help balance it out.

White can be used in every room of the house and can be combined with every color. It is common for people to paint their walls white, as the color supports all other furnishing elements in a room. Unless you are going for a very modern, sleek look, most people in their home prefer a warmer white.

- Innocence
- Purity
- Wholeness
- Perfection
- Openness

- Independence
- Calm
- Order
- Cleanliness
- Good for all rooms of the home

White Stones: Agate, Apophyllite, Calcite, Coral, Danburite, Desert Rose, Diamond, Faden Quartz, Herkimer Diamond, Howlite, Lemurian Quartz, Moonstone, Opal, Pearl, Quartz, Selenite, Topaz

Gray: Stable and elegant

Do you want stability, calmness and composure?

Gray is the color of compromise, between white and black. The darker it is, closer to black, the more mysterious it becomes, whereas the lighter it is and closer to white, the more illuminating it is.

Gray is unemotional, detached and indecisive. Because of its lack of emotion, it is solid and stable, creating a sense of calm and composure. It lacks stimulation, energy and excitement.

Gray can be conservative and boring, but also elegant and formal. It is a great color to pair with other colors because it will tone down the bright and strong colors and illuminate the softer colors. Too much gray can cause sadness and depression, so be sure to add color to counteract that effect.

Gray can be used in every room of the house if it is paired with other colors. Because it is a support color, each color that it is paired with will stand out on its own to exude that color's energy and traits.

Gray is a difficult color to use in the Pacific Northwest due to our gray days in wintertime. In geographic locations such as the Pacific Northwest where I live, where there are a lot of gray days, my recommendation is to use warmer gray tones for wall color, closer to taupe, or to combine the true gray with more intense colors to stimulate it. I love seeing gray with yellow, lime green, orange or red to give it energy. It can be beautiful and calming with blue and purple as well.

- Unemotional
- Detached
- Indecisive
- Calm
- Composed

- Stable
- Conservative
- Elegant
- Formal
- Good for all rooms of the home

Gray Stones: Agate, Calcite, Howlite, Pearl, Smokey Quartz

Black: Intrigue and sophistication

Do you want to create an air of mystery and sophistication or power and control?

Black can be a great grounding color, but only when used in moderation. It creates an air of mystery, intrigue, confidence and sophistication. It also exudes power and control, which can be intimidating and unapproachable at times. It is authoritarian.

Black is secretive and keeps things hidden from the world. It creates a barrier to the world outside your home, giving protection from external stresses. It hides vulnerabilities, lack of self-confidence and insecurities. It absorbs negative energy, as it absorbs all colors and is the absence of light. It can protect you from harm and negativity when you are outside of your home.

Due to its heaviness, it should be combined with other colors to lighten and brighten its energy. Too much black can cause depression and moodiness and create a negative environment.

You can try using black as an accent color in home décor, such as in pillows and towels, to enhance sophistication and elegance. When paired with white only, there is too much contrast, so another color needs to be used to ease the tension between the two colors.

There is a recent trend of using black paint for rooms in the home. I do not recommend this unless you are going for a heavy, cave-like feel.

- Mystery
- Confidence
- Sophistication
- Power
- Control
- Secretive
- Protective
- Good as an accent color

Black Stones: *Black Tourmaline, Chrysanthemum Stone, Garnet, Hematite, Obsidian, Onyx, Sapphire*

Brown: Stability and support

Do you want to foster stability, support and comfort?

Brown has been a design staple since the beginning of time, from light tan and beige to dark chocolate and espresso. Brown is the color of security, stability, structure and support, as well as material wealth. It is a down-to-earth color that relates to comfort and calm. Brown is a stabilizer.

Brown creates security and a sense of belonging with family and friends. This relates to emotional security, as well as to material security and the accumulation of material possessions. It also relates to physical comfort, quality and simplicity.

Brown is a friendly, approachable color and represents being loyal, trustworthy and dependable. It's honest and genuine with a feeling of being grounded. It is also practical, relating to common sense. It encourages orderliness and organization.

Some shades of brown show sophistication and elegance when they are paired with softer whites and ivories. When brown is paired with green, as it is in the outdoors, it has healing tendencies as it comforts and stabilizes, while green balances and rejuvenates, creating an environment that helps us deal with daily stresses.

Because it is a neutral, it goes well with and supports all other colors. Shades of brown used as a base create a blank canvas for design. Brown can be incorporated into every room in a home without any physiological issues. It can be seen in wood floors and cabinets, carpet, paint and more. There is a reason why "builder beige" is such a popular wall color in new construction.

- Security
- Stability
- Support
- Material Wealth
- Comfort
- Calm

- Trustworthy
- Dependable
- Grounded
- Organization
- Practical
- Good for all rooms in the home

Brown Stones: *Agate, Amber, Calcite, Desert Rose, Garnet, Jasper, Quartz, Selenite, Soapstone, Tiger's Eye*

Gold: Wealth, success and status

Do you want to create the feeling of luxury, wealth and success?

Gold is often associated with abundance, luxury, prestige and elegance. It is the color of success and achievement. It implies affluence, material wealth and extravagance.

Gold has masculine energy linked to the sun. It adds warmth and illuminates and enhances other things around it. It is associated with wisdom, understanding and enlightenment and inspires knowledge and deep understanding of the self and soul. It has been associated with royalty throughout the world.

Gold can by flashy and draw attention to itself when shiny, showing confidence and passion. Too much gold can lead one to be arrogant, overly egotistical, self-righteous and opportunistic in the quest for power.

Gold can be used in every room in the home.

UNDERSTANDING
THE SCIENCE OF
COLOR

- Abundance
- Luxury
- Prestige
- Elegance
- Success
- Material Wealth

- Extravagance
- Wisdom
- Masculinity
- Confidence
- Good for all rooms in the home

Gold Stones: Citrine, Golden Healer Lemurians, Honey Dogtooth Calcite, Pyrite, Tiger's Eye, Topaz

Silver: Illumination and reflection

Do you want to create an environment conducive to reflection and illumination?

Silver helps with reflection and changes in direction, while illuminating the way forward. It is emotional, sensitive and mysterious. It is associated with prestige and wealth, but with more glamor and sophistication compared to gold. It also has a modern, feminine appeal.

Silver has feminine energy related to the moon and the ebb and flow of the tides. It inspires intuition, clairvoyance and mental telepathy. It is soothing and calming. It helps to cleanse and release blockages and limitations as new doors open to the future.

Silver protects from outside negativity, reflecting energy back to its source. It restores stability to spiritual energy and feminine power.

Silver has a similar energy to gray, but is more optimistic. It alludes to respect, dignity, self-control, responsibility, determination and patience.

Silver works well with most other colors, illuminating and reflecting the energy of those colors. Too much silver can be dull and lifeless. It can be used in every room in the home.

- Reflection
- Illumination
- Mysterious
- Emotional
- Wealth
- Sophistication
- Intuitive
- Soothing

- Calm
- Protection
- Self-control
- Responsibility
- Patience
- Femininity
- Good for all rooms in the home

Silver Stones: *Hematite, Pearl*

Now that you have learned about the psychological and physiological sides of the colors, which ones resonate with you and your overall intentions for your Sacred Soul Space? List your overall intentions for the room here. What color or colors will help you achieve that intention? You will be able to refer back to this section when you are *Putting It All Together*.

Intention:

_____

Color(s):

_____

_____

Intention:

_____

Color(s):

_____

_____

Intention:

_____

Color(s):

_____

_____

Intention:

_____

Color(s):

_____

_____

4

Furniture: Space Planning and Feng Shui

In this section, we will review in detail the placement of major furniture pieces for specific kinds of rooms.

In the last decade, I have been in tens of thousands of homes for my home staging and interior design business. What I have seen time after time is that the majority of people have a very challenging time with space planning a room so that it is both functional and feels and looks really good. Often, there is too much stuff in a space, so it feels smaller, cluttered and claustrophobic. It is rare to see a home too bare or furnished too minimally.

The scale and balance of furniture is very important to the overall feel of a room. If the furniture is too big or there is too much of it, it makes the room feel small. Alternatively, if the furniture is too small or minimal, it can make the room feel cold and bare, with low energy.

This is particularly true in bedrooms. A lot of people have beds that are too large, which makes it harder to move around physically. Energy also has a hard time moving around the space in this case, which can create a stifled, claustrophobic feeling to the room. When energy is stifled, sleep patterns can be disrupted.

The function and purpose of a room will naturally determine what kind of furniture will go into the space. For instance, a bedroom will always have a bed at the very minimum, but will usually have accompanying nightstands and dressers. A living room will have seating. A dining room will have a table and chairs. An office will typically have a desk and a chair.

Furniture Positioning

Now it's time to talk about where to place your furniture. In all cases, it is important to arrange furniture so that the energy can flow through the room without restriction. In general, you do not want to block walkways with furniture. For example, from the doorway, you do not want to immediately walk into a piece of furniture, as it creates a wall and the energy is restricted.

Ideally, major furniture pieces should be placed in the power position. This means that when you are sitting on your sofa, lying in your bed or sitting at your desk, you can see the main door. That way you can see who is coming into the space and nothing can sneak up behind you. If it is not possible to have your furniture in the power position, there will be suggestions for alternatives in each type of room.

In this section, we will focus on the following room types: living rooms/family rooms, dining rooms, bedrooms, offices, multi-purpose rooms and spiritual/meditation rooms.

Living Rooms

Living rooms and family rooms are some of the most challenging spaces to arrange furniture in such a way that invites good feng shui energy and creates a functional conversation area and/or TV watching area. In a living room, the focal point might be a fireplace, a TV or an outside view. The scale of the furniture and the amount of furniture are crucial to making a living room look and feel its best.

At a minimum, most living rooms will have a sofa or loveseat, at least one additional chair, and a coffee table set of some sort. Larger rooms may have more furniture or larger scale furniture, such as a sectional. The size and positioning of the large pieces are important in the overall feeling of the living space, so that they don't block the walkway and make the room feel too small.

The first step is to determine the focal point of the room. Is there a fireplace? Is there a TV that needs to be seen? Does the room have an amazing view? If the room has all of these, you will need to rank the order of their importance in your space. You may be able to incorporate at least two of the three focal points, if not all. Typically if there is a TV in the room, it will have the highest priority if it is the main TV watching area in the house.

When walking into the room, avoid large pieces of furniture in front of the door. This will block energy and create a "wall". You want energy to flow easily around the room. Think about the room's natural walk pattern. Energy flows in a similar way. Consider putting the sofa (or loveseat) on or near a wall that is away from the main entry door. If you are able to see the entry to the room from the main sofa or sitting position, you've found the best place for the it, as it gives you the power position in the room. The sofa can be on a solid wall or a wall with windows. A sofa/loveseat in this position generally opens up the floor space.

Once you decide the best position for the sofa (or largest upholstered piece), the other furniture can be placed in the room accordingly, starting with the rest of the seating. If you have a loveseat and/or chairs in addition to the sofa, there are a number of configurations that can work in a room. The picture examples will give you some ideas of what you might want to do in your own Sacred Soul Space.

Once you have the seating in place, decide where the tables will go. The coffee table will look and feel its best if centered on the sofa rather than trying to center it in the room or on a rug. If you have a chair (or chairs) next to the sofa, with the two arms almost touching, it creates a triangular space between them. For the best energy, you want to fill that triangle with something, whether it is a table, a plant, a vase with sticks or something similar. An empty triangle space can create angry energy.

Typically, a side table will fit nicely in the empty space between them, providing a function to hold a lamp or a beverage, and it helps the room feel complete.

If the chairs are facing parallel to the sofa, I like to put a table between them, so that they both have access to a table for placing drinks or other items on the table, as they may not be able to reach the coffee table.

Study my pictures to understand how to best utilize the furniture you have in your own space. It may take some playing around with your furniture to see what feels best. It's amazing what moving furniture a few inches can do to a space as well.

L-Shape

A loveseat or one to two chairs can form an L-shape with the sofa. A side table sits in between the corners of the arms to fill the space. If you have enough room to have an additional side table, it is best placed on the other side of the sofa for balance. The coffee table is centered on the sofa. A rectangular or oval coffee table works best for the space because the loveseat or chair (single or duo) is shorter than the sofa.

If there are chairs instead of a loveseat, one or two chairs can form an L-shape with the sofa, with the side tables on either side of the sofa. A rectangular or oval coffee table is best for this configuration.

Parallel

In the room below, the fireplace is the focal point. The sofa and loveseat are placed across from each other in a parallel position. Side tables are split so that one is next to the sofa and one is next to the loveseat. The rectangular coffee table is placed closer to the sofa. In this situation, a square or circular table could be used to fill the middle space a little more and allow the loveseat to have access to the coffee table as well. Side tables are placed away from the fireplace, so that it doesn't look and feel too crowded.

Two chairs can be placed parallel to the sofa instead of a loveseat. In this case, two or three side tables can be used. Two tables can be placed on either side of the sofa with an additional table placed between the chairs as an option, or two tables split with one next to the sofa and one in between the chairs. You may opt not to have side tables next to the sofa.

This example only has the two side tables

flanking the sofa rather than sitting in between the chairs. The chairs have their backs to a main entryway in the room. A table sitting in between them would block the energy in the space. Without the table, energy is able to flow through the space easier and visually the chairs look lighter and more like a window rather than a solid wall.

Fireplace Flank

With a fireplace as the focal point, two chairs can flank either side with the sofa across from them. In this case the side tables would sit on either side of the sofa with the coffee table in front of the sofa. If there were tables next to the chairs in this scenario, it would be too much bulk for the space. If extra lighting is needed, standing lamps would be a good solution to this problem. This particular room has a sliding door that needs to be accessible, so having chairs away from the sofa opens up a nice walkway and balances the room.

U-Shape

In this configuration, a sofa or loveseat with two chairs can form a U-shape with the sofa. Side tables again are placed on either side to fill in the empty space between the sofa/loveseat arms and the chairs. A rectangular or oval coffee table is best for scale with this furniture position.

Chair Split

Another strategy is to have two chairs with a sofa split up, so that one chair is united with the sofa in an L-shape and the other chair is placed at an opposite diagonal to form a triangle conversation area in the room. A side table sits between the chair and the sofa with the other table next to the chair that has been separated. Alternatively, the second side table could be placed on the other side of the sofa instead of next to the separated chair.

A similar configuration is great for a sofa, loveseat, and chair combination. With the fireplace as the focal point, the sofa and the chair have the power position, as they can see the main entryway.

Odd-shaped living rooms

If your living room is extra large or an odd shape, you may want to create a second sitting area with a couple of chairs, loveseat or chaise to take advantage of the space. You don't want it to look and feel too empty. This particular room is small, oddly shaped, long and skinny, with three separate possibilities for seating. The loveseat fits on the door-side wall. It is offset from the two chairs based on the placement of the door and the solid wall with sconces across from the door. An additional chair is placed next to the

fireplace for a cozy reading spot. Fortunately for this house, there is a huge bonus room for watching TV, so this living area is for conversation only. The scale of the furniture in this space is very important. A sofa would be far too large on any of the walls, so a loveseat is used instead.

The home below has a main living area for a sofa and loveseat, and it has an additional sitting area next to the window with a view. The sofa and loveseat are oriented towards the fireplace as the focal point and open to the dining space that is adjacent to the living area. Two small chairs are placed next to the window to create a separate conversation area while taking advantage of the view. A sofa and loveseat combination were chosen for the living room so that there aren't too many chairs in the space. Four chairs would clutter the look of the room.

With some living rooms, you will not be able to avoid creating some type of "wall" or blockage with the sofa or sectional due to the focal point of the room and shape and placement of windows, doors, etc. In this case, the use of tables and other furniture pieces may need to be lightened up to create a flow for the energy. If possible, keep a large entry for people to be able to enter into the space. This may require shifting the furniture down or forward away from the door.

This particular room has a step down into the space that is narrow from the fireplace to the wood upper floor. The sofa will only fit with its back to the rest of the space rather than being on the window or the solid wall opposite the window. Only one side table on the window side can be used to create a large enough opening between the sofa and the two chairs on the wall opposite the window. The side table and sofa are moved as close the window as possible to allow the entry space to be larger. A rectangular coffee table has to be used in this space as well because of the narrowness

of the room.

In this living room, the sectional is placed floating in the middle to face the focal point of the fireplace. No side tables are placed beside the sectional to allow enough room for people to walk around the space without feeling like it is too constrictive. A chair is placed next to the fireplace for balance and extra seating, with a side table for the function of an extra surface. A rectangular coffee table is placed in front of the sectional.

In the family room below, with the focal point of the fireplace and the bump-out of the window wall, we have to position the sectional so that you walk into the back of it from the entry and formal living room. In order to create space, the sectional is moved forward to create a large entry into the room. The side table is placed directly next the window with the sectional right next to it to give as much opening into the middle space as possible.

Additional furniture pieces can be added into the room if the space allows for it. If the room is used for watching TV, it will have some sort of console table for the TV and components on a focal wall. You may have bookshelves or similar shelving that you want in the room. Every space will vary in terms of the furniture it can handle, so try out different configurations to see how they feel to you. Use your intuition to gauge the fullness of the room before you start adding the artwork and accessories. Furniture placement should be finalized before adding in art and accessories for optimal results.

Dining Rooms

At a minimum, a dining room will have a table with chairs. There might be additional pieces that fit in the space, such as a china cabinet or sideboard, but these are secondary to the main focal point of the table. Make sure that the table is an appropriate size for the space without feeling too large or too small. I love tables with leaves, so that you have the option to make the table larger if you are hosting more guests than usual.

You should be able to walk around the entire table and chairs without feeling like it is too tight. A good rule of thumb is at least three feet of space around the table, although that may not be possible in smaller rooms. The shape of the room will determine the shape of the table. In most cases, a rectangular or oval shaped table will work just fine. In some cases however, a square or round table might feel and look better in the space.

I've included some picture examples of typical rectangular dining tables. The table size varies, and some of the dining spaces have rugs to soften the space, while others have the table directly on top of the wood floor. The scale of each table fits the dining room in which they are shown, with ample room to circle the table and get in and out of the chairs. If you are going to add an area rug to the dining room, it is very important that the rug is large enough so that when the chairs are pulled out, the legs are still on the rug. Otherwise, it will create an imbalance in the chair when someone sits in it.

An oval-shaped dining table can be a great style instead of the typical rectangle. The round edges help to soften the look of the room.

Smaller dining areas and kitchen eating areas do better with round or square shaped dining tables.

When placing chairs around a round shaped table, I often like having the chairs in a diagonal X-pattern in the space rather than in a cross perpendicular placement because it allows people to get in and out of their chairs most easily in many cases. It feels more spacious and makes the area appear a little larger. Often the cross perpendicular placement has chairs backing up to doors, walls and windows, which can feel confining.

Bedrooms

In a bedroom, the bed is the focal point, so it should be the center of attention. Positioning of bedroom furniture can be tricky if the room is shaped in an odd way or there are too many windows. Read through the different scenarios to figure out the best configuration for your bedroom.

In feng shui theory, the number one priority is to have your head toward a solid wall (the solid wall behind you). A solid wall protects you and gives you security as you are sleeping. You will notice in the examples that follow that the solid wall is more important than the power position when you can't have both in your bedroom.

The size of the room will determine whether or not you can have one or two nightstands next to the bed. A room is better when it's balanced; if it is a large room, two nightstands are generally better than one, so that the bed is flanked on either side. The dresser would be positioned on the wall opposite the bed for optimal balance.

A chair or other furniture can be brought in only if the room is large enough to accommodate it, and the additional furniture is not floating in space. A chair is best placed in a corner or a nook of some sort to anchor it. A chair could also replace one of the nightstands if that provides better function for you in a smaller room such as in the bedroom below.

FURNITURE:
SPACE PLANNING
AND FENG SHUI

If the room is smaller, one nightstand can be used on one side of the bed and then balanced with the dresser on the other side, ideally with the drawers pointing towards the bed to create some space between the bed and dresser. The alternative scenario would be to have a taller dresser flanking the bed as a nightstand would if the room is really small.

The key to the positioning of furniture and the amount of furniture is all about the balance of the room. This will depend on size of the room and type of furniture that goes into the space, as well as window size and location. When you are looking at the empty floor space, once furniture is in the room, try to have near equal amounts on both sides of bed and reduce huge gaps in space from the foot of the bed to the facing wall if possible.

Bedroom Scenario 1: Positions of Power

From the door, the bed should be positioned on a solid wall where the foot of the bed is towards the door, but not directly in front of it. When you are laying in bed, you should have a direct visual of the door. This puts you in the power position; you can see what is coming at you. The solid wall behind you gives you support and security when sleeping. By having the bed offset from the door, the energy that enters the room is not overpowering to the person lying in the bed.

Option 1: Opposite Wall

The bed is on the wall directly across from door. In this room, there is not enough space for a second nightstand to be placed on the other side of the bed due to the bathroom door being so close to the bed. The dresser is opposite the bed to balance the room. *(Two views of the same bedroom pictured)*

Option 2: Adjacent Wall

The bed is on the far wall adjacent to the door wall. This bedroom is large and has enough space for two nightstands and a dresser. There is also a chair in the near right corner.

Bedroom Scenario 2

If there is not a solid wall facing the doorway (on either wall), but the wall is solid on the "door" side of the room, that is the next best place for the bed. This allows the energy to enter the room easily and move around. The downside is that the person lying in the bed is not in the best power position to see the door.

The amount of furniture again will be determined by the size of the room. If only one nightstand will fit into the room, it should be on the opposite side of the bed away from the door to allow the most energy to flow through. If the room is wide enough, two nightstands can be used if the one closest to the door doesn't block the energy.

Additional dresser placement will depend on the shape of the room and the window configuration. If at all possible, you do not want to walk into the side of a dresser as you are entering the room unless there is a lot of space between the dresser and the door. It would be better opposite the bed if the room allows.

In the room below, the solid wall is on the same wall as the entry door. The opposite wall has windows with a view. The bed is placed on the solid wall. There is a desk on the opposite side of the room away from the door. The bed is placed so that it has equal floor space on either side of it, taking the desk into consideration.

The room below has two sections: a lower area for the bed and a smaller upper area for a sitting area or office. The bed is placed on the solid wall, which is too small to accommodate a second night-stand next to the door area without feeling constrictive.

Bedroom Scenario 3

The least favored position for the bed is perpendicular to the door where the energy immediately runs into the bed and gets blocked like a wall. Unfortunately, in some cases, this is the only way the bed will work due to size and shape of the room and configuration of windows and closets.

If this is the case, the number of furniture pieces is critical to making the room feel its best. The shape of the room will dictate which remaining pieces can go where, so in some cases, one nightstand on the opposite side of the bed can be used, with a dresser at the foot of the bed. Another strategy would be to have the nightstand on the door side of the bed with the dresser on the far side of the bed if there is not space for it on other walls.

It is really important to have empty floor space for energy to flow around the bed as much as possible. Remember to balance the room so that one side doesn't look and feel "heavier" than the other side. This is easier said than done. In my opinion, it is better to situate the bed a bit further away from the door to create more space than to put it too close and feel restricted when entering the room.

FURNITURE:
SPACE PLANNING
AND FENG SHUI

The immediate picture below is a large bedroom, so it doesn't feel as bad when walking into the space as a smaller bedroom would with the same configuration and placement of furniture as seen below.

In this room the bed is pushed towards the window to open up the floor space.

Bedroom Scenario 4

What if there are no solid walls in the bedroom? What if the best wall for the bed has windows on either side of where the bed would be placed in its ideal position? This works as long as the part of the wall behind the bed is solid. Window treatments can create the illusion of a solid space so energy doesn't enter and leave the windows.

What if a bed must be positioned under or partially under a window? You will need to choose the best wall for the bed to be on, pretending the wall is solid, and then create a look that gives you the solid support you need for security. Window treatments and high headboards used individually or together can create this effect fairly well.

The bed below would need a heavy curtain behind the bed to make it work for sleeping comfortably. The other walls are too small for the bed.

This bed would also need a heavy curtain behind it to work for sleeping purposes. If possible, the bed would be better placed on the left wall that is solid rather than under the window.

If you are only using window treatments to create a "solid wall effect," they will need to be as heavy/solid looking as possible, which means that sheers are not sufficient. If the window is smaller than the bed, consider putting up a curtain rod that expands the entire width of the bed with curtain panels covering the whole rod. This creates the illusion of a full size headboard and gives your bed the support it needs.

Please note: DO NOT put your bed at an angle in the corner. It creates a triangle space behind the bed, which can generate angry energy.

Office Space

Office space planning can be a challenge depending on your desk set-up and the position of the room's windows. The best configuration puts you facing the door while sitting in your desk chair and your back to a solid wall. Facing the door gives you the power position to see what's coming at you, including money walking through the door. A solid wall gives you the support and security you need from behind.

Office Scenario 1: Power Position

These offices have solid walls directly across from the doors, so the desks have been oriented to face the door directly with the solid wall behind the desk chair for full support.

Office Scenario 2: Facing Door

If you were unable to face the door with a solid wall behind you, another option would be to have your desk against a wall where you can still see the door. By having the desk on the door wall, the sitting position at the desk allows the door to be seen so you can see what is coming. In this case, the wall opposite the desk is solid, giving it support.

Office Scenario 3: Weak Position

If your only option is to have your back to the door because of the size and shape of the room or the style of your desk, the solution is to put a mirror at eye level on the wall above your desk, so you can see what's coming into the space.

The office below really needs to have a mirror hanging above the desk, so that the person can see what's coming behind them. Without a mirror, there is no power. If possible, the desk would be better placed on the opposite wall from where it is, so that the chair is facing the door.

For this corner desk, the wall a person faces while working will determine whether or not he or she feels any power there. The left side of the desk is on the door side of the room, so the person can see the door. If using the right side of the desk, the person's back is to the door. The optimal solution to this problem is to rotate the desk, so that the desk has its right side touching the door wall and its left side floating in mid room with the chair back on the solid wall. (Rotate the desk ninety degrees clock-wise, as shown in the picture below, right.) If turning the desk were not possible, a mirror would need to be on the wall adjacent to the door, above the desk.

This office also has a view, and your back is to the door to take advantage of seeing the view. Replacing the piece of art with a large mirror would help better this situation, so that the door can be seen while seated.

This office has a water view, so the owner wants to be able to enjoy that view when sitting at the desk. This puts them in the worst position for power. One solution in this case is to place a mirror on the wall to the right of the desk and window, next to the vase with sticks, so that the door is reflected. Even with a mirror, the person sitting at the desk may not be able to see the door from that position. This in itself can be problematic because placing a mirror directly across from a door can cause the energy to leave the room as it enters, resulting in bad feng shui.

Having a mirror directly across from an entry door creates its own problems due to the mirror reflecting energy and sending it back out of the room. If this is a high-use office, the owner would need to forego the view for optimal results.

The caveat to office feng shui from my experience is that the more time you spend in your office, the more important these concepts are to creating a working environment conducive to inspiration. If you only happen to use your office for brief moments and have a great view, don't worry as much about the power position. My own office space has a view, and I have my desk on the window. I do my computer work on my laptop in the living room, so I am in a great power position when doing the majority of my work. If I used my office regularly, I would reposition my desk to have my back on the solid wall.

Offices tend to be common clutter areas due to papers and supplies. It is really important to come up with some organization system so that you file papers away regularly and have a neat, tidy place ready to be worked in. Clutter creates chaos in the mind, as we covered earlier in the manual. Papers are some of the worst clutter that people have in their homes and their offices. To create a Sacred Space within the office, the room needs to be clutter-free with furniture positioned in optimal position and meaningful items placed in the room, which we will cover later in the manual.

Multi-Purpose Rooms

Some rooms in a home have multiple purposes. The size and function of these rooms will dictate what type of furniture you will want to place in the room.

This combination room of bedroom and office has the optimal positioning of furniture for both the bed and the desk. The desk chair can see the door directly. The person sleeping can see the door from the bed as well. Both are in the power position and the bed is on a solid wall, so it has support and security.

This desk has a view of the door, so it is okay for the space. The sofa is oriented towards a TV, so while it is not optimal for the back to be to the door, it is functional for the room.

In the picture below, the desk is almost oriented correctly for pure power. It has a direct view of the door. Because of the angle of the desk, part of the chair back is on a window rather than a solid wall, so it doesn't provide as much support as if the desk were parallel the solid wall (perpendicular to the window). The sectional is positioned to be in a TV watching space, so while it is functional for the room, it is not optimal for the power position.

If you have a multi-purpose room, make sure each part of the room has enough space to dedicate what it needs to fulfill you. For instance, you may have an office plus yoga or meditation space. Because offices tend to be more easily cluttered than other spaces, make sure you have enough furniture to hide clutter in the office part, so you are not distracted when doing yoga or meditation. This is important because clutter creates chaos in the mind.

Meditation/Yoga/Spiritual Rooms

Like the other types of rooms, the size and function of these rooms will dictate the type of furniture you should place in them. If you are doing yoga, you will want a nice big open floor space, so furnishings would be positioned on the periphery rather than intruding on the middle space. If the room is for meditation or other spiritual practices, a smaller space for sitting is needed, and there can be other furniture in the room if it is multi-purpose. Shelves and dressers can be useful in these types of rooms for displaying art and décor that is inspiring, creating alters, holding books and other tools used for spiritual and yoga practices. In order to not have a cluttered, claustrophobic space, the key is to have minimal furniture.

- Determine the focal point of the room.
- Arrange furniture so that the energy can flow through the room without restriction.
- Do not block walkways with furniture from the doorway.
- Place furniture, if possible, based on the power position.
- Orient furniture with a solid wall to your back for support.
- Do not put too much furniture in the room.

FURNITURE:
SPACE PLANNING
AND FENG SHUI

Room I want to design:

_____

_____

_____

Focal point(s) of room:

_____

_____

_____

_____

Challenges to the room (if any):

_____

_____

_____

5

The Art of Wall Hangings

Now that you have determined the placement of your furniture pieces, it is time to add artwork. Both artwork and accessories are like the jewelry and accessories of a clothing outfit. They express the meaning of the room as you intend it. When designing your Sacred Soul Space, I find it easier to add the artwork before adding the accessories. Art tends to be more specific about where it fits best on the walls, unless you have a particularly large vase or statue you want to include in the room. Like the furniture, you do not want to have too much art in your space because it will become cluttered and create a chaotic feeling.

When choosing which art pieces to hang in your Sacred Soul Space, focus on content and color first and foremost. Are there pieces in your collection that inspire you or bring joy to you every time you look at them? If it is more of an abstract piece, does it have the colors that compliment the feeling you are aiming to inspire in your space based on your overall intention?

You want your art pieces to accentuate your room, rather than just fill space on a wall. It is okay to have filler pieces if needed to complete your space. They can always be replaced at a later time.

To truly finish your space with artwork, you may find that you need to purchase or make your own art to fit your intention and to have the appropriate amount on the wall.

Don't be afraid to create your own art if you don't have pieces that represent what you want. I had a recent client who loves to decorate in "sticks and leaves." We live in an area with an abundance of material to pick from outdoors, so if you are inspired by your outdoor surroundings, don't be afraid to try something new.

You can also purchase blank canvases from your local art and craft store for a very small price and paint whatever you like. Another way to create art on a budget or with unconventional items is to purchase frames and put in photographs of inspirational items. My kids have created some really

cool pieces in art class that when framed almost look gallery quality. I also have picked up smaller unframed artwork when traveling that I frame when I get back home. Placemats, fabric and decorative plates can be used as inspirational art if it has meaning to you in content, color or memories.

When hanging art, there are many ways to do it so it looks and feels good. If you have a lot of smaller pieces, but you have a large wall to cover, a gallery wall is an excellent option. The best way to do this with photographs is to make sure the frames match, so there is consistency. If you prefer a more eclectic look, you can mix and match frames as well, although it works better if your content is more consistent. I have a gallery wall in my home that is filled with plates from different countries (Mexico, Spain and Turkey). What unites them is that they are all the same shape (roughly) and type of item. The colors and patterns are different, but I made sure that I spread the colors out. I have a mirror in the same shape, so that it flows. If I get more plates over time, I can always take the mirror down (as it is filler) and put up more plates in its place. When hanging art on the walls, you will want to make sure the art is balanced with other art pieces and furniture, so there isn't too much on one side of the room compared to other sides.

When hanging your artwork, the most comfortable look and feel is to have the midpoint of the artwork at eye level. That will be a little bit different for everyone living in the home. Hang your art at eye level for a 5'6" person if the individuals in your home vary widely in height. This is the average height in the United States, and this is the guideline I follow when I stage a home. If your family is unusually tall or short, you can adjust the level accordingly. The key with hanging art is that you want to hang it at eye level, like you would see in a museum or a gallery. You do not want to have to look up too high to see artwork. The exception to this is if you have an extra tall wall. For example, if you have a piece of art meant for the space above a high fireplace mantle: go for it. You might have a wall that spans two levels of your home. With a tall wall, start the art at a comfortable level down low and extend it upward.

If you have a piece of art you want to hang above a piece of furniture, the level of hanging will depend on the piece of furniture. You don't want to have too big a gap between the furniture and the bottom of the art, unless there is a taller accessory that will be placed on top of the furniture piece.

In a bedroom, unless you have a very tall headboard, you will probably need to add art above the headboard to create a nice focal point for the room. You want the art to fit within the bed width without it being too small (6-12" of empty space on either side).

In an office, if you have a solid wall in front of you, consider hanging art a little lower than normal, so it is closer to your eye level when seated at the desk. In a dining room, you may want to keep art a little lower as well, so it is more comfortably viewed when seated.

There are more strategies that you can utilize when hanging art on your walls.

Gallery wall

Place the art on the floor and arrange it how you want it to look before hanging on your wall.

Horizontal (Even)

Place two or more pieces of art so that the topline or midpoint is even horizontally on the wall.

Horizontal (Staggered)

Place one piece of art high with the other piece low (up, down, up, down).

Vertical (Stacked)

Place two or more pieces of art in a vertical orientation on a wall, centered on a midpoint.

Vertical (Staggered)

Place art pieces vertically, right and left of center (left, right, left, right).

Mixed shapes and sizes

It is fine to mix and match different pieces of art that come in different shapes and sizes, whether they are framed, on canvas or something else.

Get creative with hanging art

Try new ways to hang your art if you are creative and want to be inspired.

How to hang art hassle-free

Hanging art in a quick and precise way is an art form in its own right. I strongly recommend purchasing a 24" level with a ruler if you don't already own one. My level is my best tool when I'm hanging art. Before you hang a piece of art, you will want to get the measurements first, unless it has a simple hook at the very top. I like to write my measurements on the back of the art so I don't have to measure multiple times.

One Nail

If the art has a wire or one hook, it only requires one nail. Measure the distance from the top of the art to the wire when the wire is pulled up, like it would be when hanging on a nail. Place your art on the wall in the exact spot you want it to hang. Make a small dot at the top of the art with a pencil. Take your level ruler and measure down the distance to the wire that you measured on your art. Make a small mark where the nail will go and hammer the nail. Hang the wire on the nail and level the art piece.

Example: Your wire measures down 5 inches. From your top mark, use your level ruler to measure down 5 inches and make a mark. That is where your nail goes.

D-rings or Two Nails

If the art has D-rings or a similar fixture, requiring two nails, you will first measure the distance between the mid-point of the D-rings (or placement of the nails). Once you have the horizontal measurement, you will measure the distance between the top of each D-ring and the top of the art. From my experience, often the two sides are not identical.

Once you have your measurements, place the art on the wall where you want it to hang. Make a small mark at the top. Use your level ruler to measure down the distance of one (or both) of the D-rings and make a small mark. From that new mark, place your level horizontally to measure the distance across to equal the total distance between the D-rings if that distance is less than or equal to your level ruler. For instance, I take the total measurement and divide by two. I place the halved number on the ruler on the midpoint mark, making sure my level bubble is centered. I make a mark on the 0" edge of the level ruler and make another mark out to the total distance. This way my art will be perfectly centered with my original placement.

Example: Both D-rings measure down 8 inches and across 20 inches. From the top of the art, you will measure down 8 inches. From that lower center point, you will place the 10-inch mark on your level ruler on the midpoint and make your mark at the zero line and the 20-inch line.

If your D-rings happen to not be at the same measurement down, once you have your two marks horizontally, you can adjust one of the marks up or down to match the measurements you took on the art.

Example: The right D-ring measures down 8 inches, the left measures down 8 ¼ inches and total distance between D-rings is 20 inches. From the top of the art, you will measure down 8 inches. From that lower center point, you will place the 10-inch mark on your level ruler on the midpoint and make your mark at the zero line and the 20" line. From the mark you made on the left side, place your level ruler on the mark and measure down an additional ¼" and make a mark. That is where your nail goes on the left side.

If your D-rings are further apart than your level ruler, find the total distance between the D-rings as above using a tape measure or your level ruler. From the lower centered mark you make, use your level ruler to place the halved distance on the center mark and with your level bubble centered, make a mark on the zero line. After that, take your level and put the zero line on the center mark then measure out the other halved distance to place your mark. If you are unsure if you did this correctly, use a tape measure to check your work before you hammer.

Example: Both D-rings measure down 8 inches and across 40 inches. From the top of the art, you will measure down 8 inches. From that lower center point, you will place the 20-inch mark on your level ruler on the midpoint and make your mark at the zero line. You will then move your level so that the zero line is on the center mark and measure out to 20 inches, making a mark. Your total distance will be 40 inches.

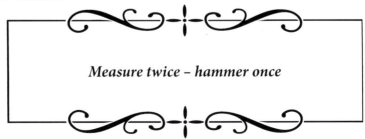

Measure twice – hammer once

6

Accessorize Your
Sacred Soul Space

What are accessories? For the purposes of designing your Sacred Soul Space, accessories are the extra finishing touches of a room that do not include furniture and wall-hanging artwork. Accessories include vases and pottery, figurines, candles, pictures, plants and flowers, rugs, curtains, bedding, pillows, blanket throws, runners, tablecloths and similar items.

When bringing accessories into your space, it is important for each piece to have some meaning for you or to complete the overall feeling of the space you are creating. You don't want objects that might hold negative energy or bad memories. You also don't want a piece in your space out of guilt because it was a gift.

There are some easy design elements to keep in mind while accessorizing. Once you are familiar with these elements, you can play around with them to see what looks and feels best for your space.

- Triangulation
- Odd Numbers
- Collections
- Greenery
- Soft Surfaces
- Lighting
- Room Corners

Triangulation

When you are placing multiple accessories on a surface top, triangulating (small, medium, large) and staggering accessories has the best look and appeal, particularly on a subconscious level. For instance, if you have three items, you will want to arrange them so that the largest item is at the back, with the small and medium items forming a three-dimensional triangle with the large item. The medium item may be placed in the back next to the large item with the small item centered in front, or the small and medium items are both placed in front, with the large item centered in the back.

The key is that you want the three items to be different in height, yet proportional in scale and size. It would look unbalanced to have a very large lamp next to a very small candle, since the scale is so different.

When you have multiple items of varying sizes on a shelf, stagger both the height and the position on the shelf in a three-dimensional way. Some items are pulled forward, with others pushed back and the heights of the items create a meandering, up and down effect.

Odd Numbers

Odd numbers of accessories are subconsciously more appealing than even numbers of accessories. For instance, if a shelf or table is on the smaller side, or your accessories are relatively large, one and three are the magic numbers rather than two and four. This is true for every single surface in a space.

The exception to this rule comes into play if you have a shelving unit with multiple surfaces. Items can be arranged in a somewhat staggered fashion to incorporate the odd number rule. For instance, you may have one large accessory on one shelf plus a grouping of two items on another shelf to create the odd number effect.

Another exception to the odd number rule is how items are configured in their grouping. If you move two pieces together in such a way that they overlap, they can create the illusion of one piece and therefore be appealing to the eye. Alternatively, if you have four or six items that are identical in size and shape, they can be lined up in a row to create a cohesive look that maintains the idea of the odd number rule because the separate pieces become one piece (i.e., candles of identical shape and size lined up along a shelf or on a fireplace mantle).

Collections

If you have a collection of items, such as vases made out of the same material or a similar color, you will create a higher impact by grouping them together rather than spreading them out. If you have appropriate shelving or a special table, arrange them so they vary in height in a meandering fashion – high – low – medium, etc.

For example, in my living room, I have large shelving units on one wall with collections from my worldly travels. On one shelf, I have grouped together all of my Raku pottery vases and arranged them in a meandering height configuration. On another shelf, I have all of my Spanish pottery of identical color and style grouped together, and I have added additional pieces that have the same look and feel. By uniting them on one shelf, they collectively form a cohesive look that cuts down on the cluttered look they would have if they were intermixed with other items with different colors and patterns.

In your own space, before you place items on surface tops, group your accessories together with how you think they might look best. Some ideas on how to group together items include:

- Similar colors
- Similar patterns
- Items from one region or country
- Similar types of items (i.e., musical instruments, candles, family pictures, books, etc.)

You can play around with how you want to group and categorize your collections to see what you like best. Once you have the items grouped together, it is time to place them on the surfaces. If you have one shelving unit with stacked, linear shelves, each grouping can be placed on a separate shelf. If you have a multiple shelf system that has horizontal and vertical shelves, like I do in my home, I like to balance the color and pattern.

For instance, if I have a shelf with light colored items on the left side of the unit, I also have similarly colored light items on the right side. To make it more interesting, I put them on different levels rather than them being at the same level on the shelves.

Bring your most beloved objects into your Sacred Soul Space if they will fit rather than keeping them in other rooms that don't have as much meaning to you.

Greenery

One way to make your Sacred Soul Space feel amazing is to bring the outside in. Add greenery. Real plants and flowers improve air quality and the overall feng shui; they bring in energy to a room. However, if you have a black thumb like me or you have animals that will eat the plants, silk plants and flowers can be used in moderation. Both real and silk soften the space. Green is a healing color, as you learned in the Color Theory section, so feel free to use it in any room you desire.

If you choose to bring in live plants to your Sacred Soul Space, there are specific plants that are known for their special properties.

Jasmine – attracts positive energy; strengthens relationships and builds romance; attracts love and money; aphrodisiac; encourages prophetic dreams; soothes stress and provides energy. Place in south-facing window.

Peace Lily – prospers spirituality both mentally and physically; improves flow of energy in home; purifies air and neutralizes harmful indoor gases. Good in bedrooms for tranquility and restful sleep; grows well in shaded or dark environments.

Bamboo – a symbol of good fortune and prosperity; attracts joy and wealth; offers protection and luck; promotes mental and physical well-being; aids in spiritual growth; helps develop artistic talents; encourages good health; influences life energy, vitality and physical activity. Place in corner of room with low lighting, away from direct sunlight.

Rosemary – promotes mental and physical well-being; purifies air to keep free of toxins; uplifts mood, reduces fatigue and anxiety; improves memory; brings inner peace; helps with sleep; attracts love and encourages lust. Prefers a sunny window.

Money Plant (*Epipremnum aureum*) – produces positive energy flow attracting good luck and fortune; reduces anxiety, stress and negative thoughts. Place in sharp corner.

Aloe Vera – bears good luck and positive energy; many healing benefits. Prefers indirect sunlight or artificial light.

Orchid – attracts positive energy and improves energy of home and lives of homeowners; attracts love; soothes the soul, deepens friendships; associated with fertility and virility. Good in a bedroom; it releases oxygen at night.

Basil – clears air of negative energy; attracts positive energy to home; antioxidant with antibacterial, anti-fungal and anti-inflammatory benefits; brings love, passion, wealth and luck. Full sun in north, east or northeastern area of home.

Chrysanthemum – represents purity and honesty; believed to have healing powers; purifies air and removes toxins from home; promotes well-being; symbolizes a long life. Place in areas with tension to provide calmness.

Sage – rids air of negative emotions, including anger and fear; brings positive energy to home; protects home; represents immortality, longevity, and wisdom; used for medicinal purposes. Keep in a humid area.

English Ivy – purifies and filters air; promotes serene, stress-free home.

Areca Palm – softens the energy of a home; purifies air.

Honeysuckle – offers protection; brings money into home; boosts psychic powers; sharpens intuition.

Lemon – symbolizes purification and friendship; brings brightness and happiness into space.

Lavender – elevates mood; calms and relaxes; helps with sleep; helps alleviate headaches.

Miniature Roses – attracts love, healing and luck; offers protection; helps with divination of all kinds. Each rose color has its own meaning:

> White – purifying and healing, positive energy

> White with red details – passion and devotion

> Peach – peace, spirituality and friendship

> Pink – romantic love, sweetness, fun, play

> Fuchsia – lust for life, self-love, deep love and acceptance of physical body

> Lavender – spirituality

> Red – passionate, deep, true love

Soft Surfaces

Rugs

To truly make a room feel its best, it is important to combine hard and soft surfaces so there is balance. If you have hard surface floors, such as wood, concrete, laminate or tile, adding rugs in key areas will really help the space feel warm and cozy. The size of each rug is crucial for the balance of the room.

Typically in a living room, the minimum rug size for a sofa/loveseat or sofa/two chair combination is five by seven feet. The rug should touch the legs of the sofa or have a little bit under the legs to anchor the furniture. You don't want your rug floating like an island in the middle of the floor with a coffee table on it, if at all possible. You may decide that you want more surface area covered with a rug for comfort purposes, so adding in a larger rug is always okay. The main thing is to stay away from a rug that is just too small for your living space. It will look strange and feel unbalanced.

If the rug is for a bedroom, the size will depend on how much of the floor you want to cover. If you want to be able to step onto the rug when you are getting out of bed, a larger rug will be necessary. If the rug is only to soften the space and add color and texture, a five by seven foot rug may be sufficient. With a smaller rug, I recommend placing the wider part of the rug under the foot of the bed, with at least half of the rug exposed depending on the size of the room.

For rugs in dining rooms, proportion and rug type is important esthetically and functionally. You need a rug that is easy to move chairs back and forth on, so a tightly woven, low pile rug is more functional than a softer, high-pile shag rug. The rug needs to be large enough to fit under your table and chairs such that when you pull a chair out to sit on it, the rug is still under the chair so as not to be off-balance with two feet on the rug and two feet off the rug.

Rug color and style will come down to personal taste. I am a textile and visual person, so I want my rugs to feel good and look beautiful. If you have highly patterned furniture or bedding, I recommend a rug with a subtle pattern, if any. If you would like to combine patterns, the rug pattern needs to be either significantly larger or smaller than the pattern on the furniture or bedding, so it doesn't compete for attention. Combining patterns can be tricky, but the general rule of thumb is to mix and match small, medium and large patterns, while maintaining a fairly consistent color scheme within the patterns.

What about rooms with carpet? Should you add a rug? This is for you to decide as you consider the functionality of your home and the look you want it to have. Rugs can add color and texture to otherwise boring space, so I am all for putting a rug on top of carpet if it adds to the room.

Curtains/window treatments

Curtains, draperies and valances are excellent additions to soften a window and add color to a room. Even if your window has existing blinds or shades, adding side panels will pull together a finished look.. Draperies tend to be much more expensive to install, so unless you really like the heaviness and function of a drapery, I recommend keeping your window treatments simpler.

With the least amount of fabric, valances are a good choice for simplicity. The valance can cover the top portion of the window only (traditional valance, pictured left), or they can flow more broadly across the top and down the sides (scarf valance, pictured right). In my experience, the flowing style is more limited in color selection. A traditional valance topper can be custom made easily in any fabric. If store bought, you will find more patterned selections.

ACCESSORIZE
YOUR SACRED
SOUL SPACE

Adding full-length (to the floor) side panels is the most common way to soften a window in a relatively inexpensive way. You can install a single metal curtain rod above the window with decorative finials extending on either side.

Alternatively, you can add two shorter panel rods on each side of the window (for extra large windows), overlapping the window itself and the wall, with panels hanging down from each.

My general rule of thumb when hanging curtain rods is to have the outer bracket at least three to four inches outside the window and a similar distance above the window. The top placement of the rod will depend on any existing window trim and the length of the panels being used. If you want the windows to appear larger, extend the brackets even further outside the windows. This will allow the panels to stack mostly outside the window area and bring in as much light as possible.

The curtain panels can be any fabric, weight, color and style that appeal to you personally and flow with the overall look of the room. You may

want panels with patterns or multiple colors, or you may prefer to keep the panels a solid color for simplicity.

The length of the panels will depend on the height of your particular window. Standard windows in homes allow for 84-inch curtain panels. Some of the newer homes I work in have much taller windows, which require 96-inch or even longer panels. Measure the height of your windows before

shopping so you purchase the correct size. Ideally the bottom of the curtain panel will skim the floor.

For a home you are living in, you don't want the curtains to have a "high-water" look if at all possible. You may have to special order curtains if you require the longer size, as a lot of stores will only carry on premise the

standard 84-inch size. Here is a picture of the "high water" look with the curtain panels.

This is what curtain panels should look like when hung *(pictured left)*.

I'm not a fan of the 63-inch curtains that fall just below a window without extending to the floor. However, if you have a wall heater under the window, this may be your only choice for safety purposes.

🌿 Step 1: Measure the width of window. You want a rod that extends several inches beyond the window.

🌿 Step 2: Measure the height of the window from the floor. You should purchase curtain panels that will skim the floor when the rod is hung above the window.

🌿 Step 3: Decide what type of curtain panels you want to add to your space. The number of panels will depend on how much of the window area you want to cover. If you only want to add softness, two panels (one on each side) will suffice. If you have a larger window, it may take at least four panels to get full coverage when they are closed. Each panel package will indicate the width of the panel, so pay attention to the panel width and your total window width when purchasing. Every curtain panel design will be slightly different in its width.

Bedding

In a bedroom, the largest area of soft surface is the bed, with its blankets and pillows. Choosing your bedding can have a high impact on the overall feeling of your Sacred Bedroom Space. Think carefully about the colors and energy you want to bring into your bedroom space before you purchase bedding. Do you want a peaceful, relaxing space? Blues and greens are great colors to bring in. Do you want joy, energy and inspiration? Bedding with yellows and oranges would be good to bring in. Is it passion you want to create? Red is the color for you, but only in moderation.

Patterns on bedding can affect your overall well-being in your bedroom as well. Make sure you really love the pattern and that it will fit well in your space.

Throw pillows, discussed more below, are a great addition to a bedding set to accentuate specific colors. They can coordinate and flow with the bedding or they can be a sharp contrast for a more dramatic look.

Pillows and throw blankets

Adding pillows and throws to wood furniture will soften them, particularly if there is a lot of hard surface in the room already. Pillows and throws add color and texture and can be a great way to add contrast and bring in the physiological and psychological benefits you want to foster in your Sacred Space.

If you have neutral colored furniture, pillows are a way to bring in color. Alternatively, if you have boldly colored furniture, neutral pillows and throws can balance the color.

The quantity of pillows will be a personal choice. I typically put one pillow on each chair and four to five pillows on sofas. If there is a sofa and loveseat combination, I might put three to four pillows on the sofa and two pillows on the loveseat.

Pillows are a great way to bring in patterns or meaningful concepts. As an example, I have two pillows in my living space that feature two of my favorite animals: manta ray and elephant.

Runners and tablecloths

When you have a wooden or hard surface table top on hard surface floors, you may want to soften those spaces by using runners or tablecloths. For instance, in a dining room that has hardwood floors, you can soften the "wood on wood" look by using a table runner for a minimal look or a tablecloth for more full coverage. When you have a wooden eating table on top of wooden floors with nothing to break up the wood, it subconsciously feels hard and unwelcoming. Adding runners or tablecloths is a great way to add color and texture as well as enhance the warmth of your space overall.

You may choose to add a runner to other types of tables as well for similar reasons. A runner, or even a placemat, on top of a bedroom dresser or a side table can add a nice touch of color and soften the hard surface.

Lighting

Lighting in your Sacred Soul Space can have a huge effect on the overall feeling and look of your room. The type of lighting you will need depends on the function of the room. If you are in a room where you need to do detailed, artistic work, bright lighting will be needed. If you want a reading space, a bright lamp to aid reading is required. You may want to include different kinds of lighting to set different moods in the room. This can include an overhead light, table lamps, standing lamps, and other kinds of lamps that produce direct and indirect lighting, including salt lamps.

If your overhead lighting is an important part of the type of room you are designing, such as a dining room, a beautiful chandelier or similar type of hanging fixture can transform a room and make it unique to you and your space. Changing out a light fixture is an easy way to transform the look of a space with a little bit of money.

There are many styles, colors and shapes of lamps to choose from, so you can have fun when choosing the lighting to add to your space. Even something as simple as changing the shade of a lamp you already own can have a dramatic shift in how you view your room.

If you decide to install a dramatic hanging light fixture, make sure there is a piece of furniture under it, so as not to be in the direct walk-path where you or others will hit your head. A chandelier in a dining room or kitchen eating area is best centered over the table. If you put a chandelier or a similar fixture in your bedroom, make sure it hangs over the bed or hangs high enough to not interfere with walking. The last thing you want to do is hit your head!

Room Corners

Empty corners in rooms can stagnate the energy flow. It is okay to have some corners that are empty. However, to help the energy keep flowing, I recommend having some corners with plants, trees and vases with sticks or grasses. Standing lamps and chairs can be placed in corners if you want them for function.

Adding accessories to your space is like adding jewelry to your outfit. The look and feel of the room will change as you add in or take away certain accessories. Play around with these new concepts in your Sacred Soul Space until it feels right to you. And have fun!

ACCESSORIZE
YOUR SACRED
SOUL SPACE

7

Enhance the Energy and Meaning of Your Sacred Soul Space

There are many different ways to enhance a room's energy and meaning that truly make your Sacred Soul Space special for you. In this chapter, we cover different elements you may want to incorporate into your space for a multi-sensory effect. By no means do you have to add all of the elements discussed, but there may be some new ideas that really speak to you. You may learn ways to add powerful meaning to your space and to make it unique.

The additional elements we will cover include:

- Stones/Crystals
- Meaningful Imagery
- Altars
- Vision Boards
- Essential Oils

Stones/Crystals

Stones and crystals each have their own energy and meaning, so having specific pieces in your room can add to the power of your Sacred Soul Space. Crystals hold their own energy, and they also pass along energy as conduits.

Crystals have been an important part of human culture since the beginning of our existence. They can be used individually or together, depending on the desired outcome. Crystals can be used as accessories to decorate side tables and shelving if they are substantial enough in size. They can also be used on altars. Don't be afraid to try new things with your crystals.

For a list on some of the most common crystals with their meanings and the colors you can find them in Appendix 1: Stones/Crystals.

Now think about which crystals you might want to add into your Sacred Soul Space, and list them here.

Crystals/Stones I want to incorporate into my space:

_____

_____

_____

_____

Meaningful Imagery

One way to truly personalize your Sacred Soul Space is to add in artwork and accessories that represent images that have meaning to you. This could be artwork that shows particular landscapes and scenery, such as the ocean, a forest, a meadow, a waterfall or similar. It could be artifacts that you've collected from special places you have visited. It could be objects or pictures that inspire you or make you happy, such as a particular type of vehicle (car, motorcycle, boat or similar). It could be animals that you love and inspire you.

Think about what kind of imagery you want to add to your Sacred Soul Space and list some ideas here:

_____

_____

_____

_____

In my own personal Sacred Soul Space, I have a lot of artwork and accessories that are reminders of my travels from around the world. I also have an abundance of items that represent different animals that resonate with me. As a former zoologist, I have always loved animals. In recent years, I have become more aware of the spiritual significance of these different animals. Having them in my Sacred Soul Space reminds me of their powers and characteristics and helps me navigate through life more easily.

Are there any animals that consistently come to you in your dreams or meditations? Are there any animals that you absolutely love and aren't sure why? If so, there is a really good chance it is one of your spirit allies.

Research the spiritual meaning of an animal to see if it resonates with you. There are several good books on the meaning of animals, including *Animal Speak* by Ted Andrews, *Animal Messengers* by Regula Meyer and *Pocket Guide to Spirit Animals* by Dr. Steven Farmer. You can also go online to look at different websites to see what they say about your animal.

I have found for myself that when I understand what the animal stands for, I know immediately if it is one of my allies. There may be different animals that you can call upon for different situations.

You can also research different animals and choose an animal that you want to inspire you. Recently, I was sharing with a group of women about my spiritual relationship with animals. One of the women said she really liked what I said about the platypus.

There are particular animals that represent what you are trying create, so you can bring their energy into the space with images or statues. There may be animals that speak to you for a certain time and purpose and then fade away. You may have new ones that come to you. Recently, I had a new animal come to me in the form of a swan.

If you are placing animals in certain rooms, make sure that their energy is appropriate for the space they inhabit. You don't want a really high-energy animal to be in your bedroom, as it could disrupt sleep.

To give you an example of what this might look like, my particular animals include elephant, manta ray, platypus, koala, dolphin, peacock, giraffe, dragon and swan. I have other animals around my house, but these are the most prominent and numerous in my collection of artwork, accessories and jewelry. My animals are featured on throw pillows, in artwork and as figurines/statues.

Examples of spiritual meanings of animals

These are a compilation of meanings from different books and websites.

Elephant – maternal, harmony in the herd, leadership in the tribe, strong yet compassionate, gentle, wise, focused power and strength, reconnection to our feminine attributes, connection to ancient wisdom, confidence, patience, commitment, communication in relationships, intelligence, discernment, royalty, longevity of life, happiness, ease, and good luck

Manta ray – graceful strength and wisdom, navigate emotional highs and lows without stressing too much, smooth journey, use energy and presence to direct the course of life and draw in what is desired (like a vortex), manifestation, allowing others to support and assist us, empathic – learning to build strong personal boundaries, stability and security in life, trusting your intuition, adapting to new environments easily, courage, awareness

Platypus – adaptability, ancient lessons, curiosity, connection, electricity, swim through emotions, inner sight/intuitive, hardworking, intelligent, investigation, isolation/solitude, mystery, paradox, uniqueness, acceptance and pride of not fitting in with the crowd, balance of life energies and looking for the deeper meaning of life, good at communication and expression of oneself, imagination and logic, sensitive, lighthearted, spontaneous, moving with creative ebbs and flows of earth; females have protection through their connection to spirit and their self-worth

Koala – calmness, relaxation, concentration, meditation, connection, empathy, magic, memory, protection, rest, trust, power of yoga, slow movement, friendly, amicable, nurturing maternal instinct, patience, psychic powers, focused

Dolphin – harmony, balance, communication, protection, resurrection, playfulness and joy, deep inner strength, cooperation, intuitive, trusting of instincts, self-confidence, multi-dimensional wisdom and intelligence, self-love, willpower, virtue, teamwork, courtesy, humor

Peacock – self-love, honor, integrity, facing life and unknown with courage and confidence, light-heartedness and laughter, rejuvenation, beauty, balance, wise vision, awakening, immortality, spirituality, royalty, self-confidence, leadership, resurrection/rising out of the ashes (like the Phoenix), patience, benevolence, compassion, kindheartedness, embracing inner truth, showing true colors, ability to see into the past, present and future, sexuality, longevity, expansiveness, watchfulness

Giraffe – rising above earthly matters, seeing the bigger pictures while remaining grounded, ability to see into the future, safety and strength in times of need, distinctiveness and individuality, trusting instincts, seeking the best in life, foresight, vision, intuition, ability to perceive untruths and deception, quiet contemplation, graceful movement, beauty, patience, cleverness, protection, intelligence, communication, associated with water

Dragon – self-power, achievement, success, prosperity, abundance, magic, wisdom, truth, wondrous possibility, belief in magic, hidden realms, hungering for new adventure, strength, courage, fortitude, psychic ability, transformation, metaphysical knowledge, beauty, inspiration, longevity, protection, leadership, fulfillment of potential, personal happiness, fortune, growth, luck, development, clear sight, fearless, passionate, not afraid of change, speaking truth, desire to rise above all circumstances, sense of humor, nobility

Swan – purity, beauty, grace, love, elegance, divination, balance, fluidity, creativity, depth, intuition, future vision, calm, gentle, full of hope, self-esteem, gracefully gliding through water, moving through the currents of life, awakening, clairvoyance, partnership, power, spiritual evolution, transformation, union

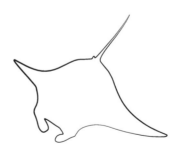

When all of the meanings are displayed in front of you, you may start to see patterns and commonality in some of the animals that you love. With my animals above, you can see that they share many similar qualities:

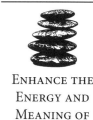

Intuition/psychic vision/clairvoyance – manta ray, platypus, koala, dolphin, peacock, giraffe, dragon, swan

Intelligence – elephant, platypus, dolphin, giraffe

Wisdom – elephant, manta ray, koala, dragon

Adaptability/transformation – manta ray, platypus, dragon, swan

Unique/authentic – platypus, peacock, giraffe

Self-love/worth/esteem – platypus, dolphin, peacock, swan

Lighthearted – platypus, dolphin, peacock, dragon

Strength/power – elephant, manta ray, dolphin, giraffe, dragon, swan

Confidence/courage – elephant, manta ray, peacock, dragon

Gracefully moving through life and emotions – manta ray, platypus, koala, giraffe, swan

Manifestation – manta ray, dragon

Patience – elephant, koala, peacock, giraffe

Spirituality – peacock, dragon, swan

Longevity – elephant, peacock, dragon

Communication – elephant, platypus, dolphin, giraffe, dragon

Happiness – elephant, dolphin, dragon

Good luck/fortune – elephant, dragon

Royalty/nobility – elephant, peacock, dragon

Beauty – dragon, swan

Maternal instinct – elephant, koala

Now, take some time to jot down the animal or animals that really speak to you. Are there animals that you loved as a child? Are there animals you love now? Take a look around your home and office and see if there are any animals that appear in your artwork and décor. If you have been on guided meditative journeys, are there any animals that have come to you? Any of these animals, mythical or real, can be used for inspiration.

Once you have figured out your significant animal(s), research their meanings. I recommend doing an Internet search and looking at several websites to put together the best meaning for you in your life. When I do this, I type in "spiritual meaning of . . . (animal)." Use your intuition. What characteristics do the animals have that really resonate with you? Write down the meanings here. Decide if that animal represents what you want to be reminded of in your Sacred Soul Space, or even in other areas of your home or office.

My Inspirational Animal(s):

Animal: _____

Meaning: _____

_____

Animal: _____

Meaning: _____

_____

Animal: _____

Meaning: _____

_____

Animal: _____

Meaning: _____

_____

Animal: _____

Meaning: _____

_____

Altars

Altars have traditionally been found in Eastern cultures as well as in some Christian sects. With yoga and meditation practices on the rise in Western society, altars are growing more popular. The purpose of creating an altar is to reinforce the intentions of your Sacred Soul Space by calling in spiritual energies. What do you want to invite into your space? Peace, serenity, love, abundance, healing or something else? Altars can be used for meditation, prayer or just as a beautiful reminder of what your Sacred Soul Space is dedicated to and your connection to the Divine Source.

The first step is to find a location for your altar in your Sacred Soul Space. It could be in a corner, on top of a table or dresser or even on a bookshelf. Use your intuition to figure out where you want the altar to be located.

Next, decide on what the theme or themes will be for your altar. Inspiration can come from the overall intention you set for the room already. Some examples of altar themes include meditation, inspiration, relaxation, healing, peace, strength, love, joy and abundance.

 Once you have decided on the intention, select objects with meaning for the altar. Examples of things to include would be a light source, such as a candles or a salt lamp; fresh flowers or herbs; inspirational books; crystals/stones; photos of loved ones or spiritual figures; elements from nature (shells, rocks, feathers, coral, sticks, etc.) and bells or chimes. Hold the object in your hand to see if it speaks to you about belonging on the altar. Only use items that resonate the energy you want to create.

Now that you have chosen your objects, it is time to arrange them in the altar space. If using a flat surface, such as a table, place the taller items in the back with shorter objects in the front. You can use triangulation patterns that were taught in the accessory section of this manual. Rearrange until you are happy with the position of the objects.

The final step is to bless the altar by saying words of gratitude or a prayer. It does not have to be long. The most important thing is the intention you are infusing into your altar with your thoughts.

Once you have the altar set up and blessed, use it in a daily ritual to enhance its energy. Over time, you will be compelled to shift items around on your altar and even change the objects that make it up. Trust your intuition. You will know when it is time for modification.

ENHANCE THE ENERGY AND MEANING OF YOUR SACRED SOUL SPACE

Vision Boards

Creating a vision board that helps you visualize your goals and dreams daily is a powerful tool of manifestation. Having a vision board in your Sacred Soul Space energizes the space with your intentions even more powerfully. When you are in your space looking at your board, you are able to generate more energy toward your dreams, so that they become reality.

If you have not had the opportunity to create a vision board, it is actually quite simple. Boards can be made for your overall intention in all areas of your life, as well as for specific areas, such as health/wellness, career/money or love/relationships. Decide if your vision board will be general or specific.

You will need a few materials to create your vision board. A thick poster board is used as the base. You can determine if a small or large board will work best for your dreams. I personally like the large ones, so that I can fit more images onto the space. Glue sticks work really well for gluing the images onto the board.

Using magazines, pictures and other paper-based materials, cut or tear out words and images that symbolize your dreams, what you want to manifest and how you want to feel. If you don't have a pile of magazines at your disposal, you can ask to borrow from friends and relatives if they have desired titles and are okay with you tearing them up. You might need to purchase some magazines that have the types of words and images that speak to you. You can also find images on the Internet to print out for use.

Once you have your images and words ready, it is time to place them on the board. Some people like to pre-place everything before they start gluing. Other people glue as they go. There is no right or wrong way to do this. The key is that you are able to see all of your intentions, so make sure you don't cover up words with larger images. You can layer the words onto the images. Having some empty space is okay. I like using a poster board that has some color in the background that is inspirational, so that if I do end up with a bit of empty space, the background color fills it. My current vision board is sparkly gold.

If you are creating a vision board with multiple intentions, consider segmenting certain areas of the board for particular areas of your life. You can be as organized as you like or as abstract and random as you like. Again, there is no wrong way to do this. Trust your intuition on how to create your board for your ultimate outcome.

Creating a vision board can be done once a year or several times a year. Do what calls to you. The time and focus that goes into creating your board helps you to hold your intention in your mind's eye during the process.

Once you have your board completed, hang it in a prominent place in your Sacred Soul Space where you will see it daily. The more time your mind spends taking in the images on the board, the more likely your subconscious mind is to call your desires into being.

Essential Oils

Essential oils have been around for thousands of years, but they have recently regained their popularity among the public thanks to companies such as doTerra and Young Living. Diffusing oils into your Sacred Soul Space can help you create a multi-sensory experience in your room. There are many different types of oils that work differently on your emotions and moods, so you will need to figure out which oils work best for what you want to experience.

For your Sacred Soul Space, I recommend diffusing the oils with an oil diffuser. You can use oils separately or together. Typically, you will only need a few drops of oil in the diffuser to produce a beautiful olfactory environment.

There are some books that go into great detail about what each of the major oils does to the emotions and how they act as healing agents. The list of oils in the appendix of this book will give you a good overview and a starting place to figure out which oils you may want to use in your space. I also encourage you to research for yourself.

The information on essential oils was garnered from two different books: *Modern Essentials: A Contemporary Guide to the Therapeutic Use of Essential Oils* published by Aroma Tools, and *Emotions & Essential Oils: A Reference Guide for Emotional Healing* by Enlighten.

If you are interested in more detailed information on the science of how essential oils can be used to help your overall health and emotional well-being, I highly recommend both as reference books.

For a list of essential oils and their properties, please see Appendix 2: Essential Oils.

Some essential oil companies have created oil blends that have specific properties and uses that you may find easier to use than trying to mix your own. These include:

- Comforting Blend
- Encouraging Blend
- Focus Blend
- Grounding Blend
- Inspiring Blend
- Invigorating Blend

- Joyful Blend
- Reassuring Blend
- Renewing Blend
- Restful Blend
- Uplifting Blend

Below are some common emotional and health issues, with the oils that can be used to help:

ADD/ADHD – vetiver, focus blend, restful blend

Addictions/Alcoholism – black pepper, lavender, rosemary, cleansing blend, restful blend

Alertness – peppermint

Anxiety – lavender, orange, lemon, copaiba, neroli, blue tansy, restful blend, , reassuring blend, encouraging blend, focus blend, massage blend, joyful blend, grounding blend, respiratory blend

Appetite Suppressant – grapefruit, metabolic blend

Calming – lavender, ylang ylang, Melissa, blue tansy, cedarwood, arborvitae, focus blend, restful blend

Chronic Fatigue – peppermint, basil, protective blend

Concentration – lavender, lemon, petitgrain, focus blend

Confusion – frankincense, sandalwood, grounding blend

Crying – ylang ylang, lavender, Roman chamomile

Depression – lemon, frankincense, lavender, bergamot, petitgrain, encouraging blend, uplifting blend, joyful blend, grounding blend, invigorating blend

Energizing – Siberian fir, peppermint, joyful blend, grounding blend

Grief/Sorrow – lemon, lavender, joyful blend, grounding blend

Insomnia – lavender, orange, spikenard, Roman chamomile, restful blend

Memory – rosemary, peppermint

Mental fatigue – frankincense

Physical stress – lavender, bergamot, geranium, marjoram, restful blend

Relaxing – lavender, ylang ylang, lemon, neroli, massage blend

Sleep – lavender, restful blend

Stress – lavender, lemon, ylang ylang, neroli, petitgrain, focus blend, joyful blend, restful blend, reassuring blend, comforting blend

Tension – lavender, ylang ylang, restful blend, massage blend

Uplifting – lemon, petitgrain, orange, joyful blend

What oils might you want to add to your space? List them here.

_____

_____

_____

_____

8

Putting it All Together

Now that you are armed with knowledge about clearing your space, color theory, space planning and feng shui energy with furniture, hanging artwork, adding accessories, and enhancing your Sacred Soul Space, it is time to put all of the information together to design your room. I highly recommend designing only one room at a time, so you can clearly focus on the intent you want to create. Once you have gone through the process of designing one Sacred Soul Space, you can use the concepts repeatedly to design different spaces with different intentions.

For example, in your bedroom, you may want to create a peaceful, relaxing space to rejuvenate while sleeping. In your living room, you may want an energized room that stimulates conversation. In your office, you may want to enhance your creativity and imagination or build trust with your clients. In your meditation or spiritual space, you may want to boost your connection with the universe. All of these intentions would include different colors and finishing touches.

Before you start the design process, I want you to take another journey into your Sacred Soul Space. Your journey may be similar to the one at the beginning of the manual or it may be drastically different. Closely focus on the details and elements that are in your Sacred Soul Space. Experience how you feel in the space. This will help you when you are pulling together your room.

Now that you have gained knowledge in many areas, take yourself on a journey within your Sacred Soul Space. You may want to record yourself reading the following text aloud to play back, so that you can be truly immersed in your journey.

Journey for Creating Space

Get yourself into a comfortable, relaxed position. Close your eyes and take several deep breaths, allowing your mind and body to relax. Melt into the surface below you. Allow yourself to go deeper and deeper into your subconscious mind. You are safe. You are secure. All is well. Become one with your breath. Become one with your surroundings.

Now that you are relaxed, in your mind's eye, transport yourself to a place in nature where you feel safe and secure. Notice your surroundings. Where are you? What images do you see? What sounds do you hear? What scents do you smell? Take some moments to fully be present in your surroundings. (Pause)

As you are immersed in nature, comfortable, taking in your surroundings, you notice a mist start to form in the distance. The mist becomes thicker and thicker as it starts rolling towards you. You know this mist is safe. The mist comes closer and closer to you and finally surrounds you where you cannot see anything. You only feel that you are safe and secure within the mist.

As the mist is twirling around you, a door appears in the distance. You walk toward the door, knowing that on the other side of the door is your very own Sacred Soul Space. You open the door and step inside, looking down at your feet.

As you slowly lift your head, you are able to see what kind of room you are in within your home or office. Which room are you in? Which colors do you see? What kind of furniture is in the room? Notice any particular pieces of artwork that stand out. Take a look at the details of the accessories. What type of fabrics and soft surfaces are in the room? Pay attention to any particular smells that are wafting through the air. How do you feel being there? Take some time to walk around this room, noticing the fine details. (Pause)

Is there anything that you want to change in your Sacred Soul Space? Is there anything that you want to add? If so, do it now. You can create this space to be anything you want it to be. (Pause)

When you feel like you have noticed the details of the space, leave the room and come back to the here and now.

Take a few moments to write down your thoughts about what you saw in the space. Try to be as detailed as you can. Write down the colors you noticed and where they were throughout the room. What kind of furniture did you see? What was special about it? What artwork and décor were present in the room? What smells were in the space? Was the room the same as your beginning journey or was it different?

PUTTING IT ALL
TOGETHER

_____

_____

_____

_____

_____

_____

_____

PUTTING IT ALL
TOGETHER

1. Choose the Sacred Soul Space that you want to design.

2. Identify your intention for the room.

3. Declutter & smudge the room.

4. Choose key colors.

5. Arrange the furniture.

6. Add artwork to walls.

7. Add accessories.

8. Add in final touches.

Room #1

Sacred Soul Space I want to design:

_____

_____

_____

Intention for Room

Identify your intention(s) for the room. What is the overall feeling you want to create? For example: calm, peaceful, relaxing, healing, inspiring, joyful, passionate, spiritual, trusting, secure, invigorating, etc. List the intentions below:

_____

_____

_____

_____

_____

_____

Colors for Room #1

Choose the colors you want to incorporate into the room to give you the feeling and intention you want to create. Your room can incorporate a few intentions, as long as they are compatible with each other rather than conflicting. For instance, if you are trying to create a peaceful, calming space, you might use blue and green, but you would not use red with those colors, unless it is in a very minimal way.

Determine how much of each color you might want and make a preliminary plan as to where and how you will use those colors (wall color vs. artwork, accessories or furniture).

For a big, bold look, use color on the walls in addition to the furnishings. For a subtle look, use a neutral color on the walls and bring in color with furnishings and accents. If you know you have very colorful art and accessories to use in the space, a neutral background can provide a nice backdrop to the main focal points in the room. Too much color can be chaotic and confusing and actually hide focal pieces.

All rooms will need a neutral color somewhere to ground everything for an optimal feel and look. This could be in the flooring, wall color or furniture.

Adding in color can be one of the most challenging design elements for you to do, but if you use your intuition, you will know how much of each color to incorporate. You might need to experiment and change things around to get the desired effect.

Paint is one of the easiest and least expensive ways to change the look of a room with a huge impact. Unless you are using a truly neutral color (like beige, cream or white), pick your paint color based on the furniture, artwork or bedding (if in a bedroom) that will be in the Sacred Soul Space. Keep in mind that different colors have different psychological and physiological emotions they evoke, as we've already covered, so choose color according to the type of room you are designing. If you are going to paint your room, do this before you add anything back into the room.

Accessories, particularly the soft surface accessories like rugs, curtains and pillows are an easy way to add in colors.

Colors I want to incorporate in my room include:

Add Furniture

Arrange the furniture so it is conducive to the optimal movement and energy patterns discussed in chapter four, while taking into account special features of the room.

Draw a rough schematic of your room, including windows and doors. With a pencil, draw how your furniture might fit within the room (roughly to scale). Draw a few different scenarios if your room is challenging. When in doubt, try it out (in person). Don't be afraid to try a few different placements of furniture in your space to find the configuration that feels the best and allows for the most energy to flow. Your furniture must be in place before you add other elements.

PUTTING IT ALL
TOGETHER

Hang Artwork

Add artwork to your walls. The placement of art will depend on furniture location and wall size. As a reminder, you want to make sure there is a good amount of space around each piece of art or collage of art on a wall so it doesn't feel too crowded. Unless there is a tall piece of furniture that you will be placing artwork above, hang artwork so that the midpoint is at roughly 5'6" (for the most comfortable look and feel). Before you hang any of the pieces, decide where each of them will go. Make sure they all fit where they need to and they look good together. Adjust as needed before you start hammering. If you have a vision board you want to include in the space, treat the board as a piece of artwork, so that it has its own special space on a wall.

Artwork I want to hang:

Add in Accessories

Now that artwork has been placed, accessories will complete the overall look of the design. If a table is small, use the triangulation method with three items maximum. Add in pillows, curtains and rugs. Are there any plants you want to bring into the space? Rearrange as needed until you like the look of what you have created.

Accessories I want to add:

_____

_____

_____

_____

_____

_____

_____

Add Final Touches

Crystals/Stones:

_____

_____

_____

Meaningful Imagery:

_____

_____

_____

Altar:

What is the location of the altar?

_____

What is the theme of the altar?

_____

Vision Board:

_____

_____

Essential Oils:

_____

_____

Sacred Soul Space I want to design:

_____

_____

_____

Intention for Room

Identify your intention(s) for the room. What is the overall feeling you want to create? For example: calm, peaceful, relaxing, healing, inspiring, joyful, passionate, spiritual, trusting, secure, invigorating, etc. List the intentions below:

_____

_____

_____

_____

_____

_____

Colors for Room #2

Choose the colors you want to incorporate into the room to give you the feeling and intention you want to create. Your room can incorporate a few intentions, as long as they are compatible with each other rather than conflicting. For instance, if you are trying to create a peaceful, calming space, you might use blue and green, but you would not use red with those colors, unless it is in a very minimal way.

Determine how much of each color you might want and make a preliminary plan as to where and how you will use those colors (wall color vs. artwork, accessories or furniture).

For a big, bold look, use color on the walls in addition to the furnishings. For a subtle look, use a neutral color on the walls and bring in color with furnishings and accents. If you know you have very colorful art and accessories to use in the space, a neutral background can provide a nice backdrop to the main focal points in the room. Too much color can be chaotic and confusing and actually hide focal pieces.

All rooms will need a neutral color somewhere to ground everything for an optimal feel and look. This could be in the flooring, wall color or furniture.

Adding in color can be one of the most challenging design elements for you to do, but if you use your intuition, you will know how much of each color to incorporate. You might need to experiment and change things around to get the desired effect.

Paint is one of the easiest and least expensive ways to change the look of a room with a huge impact. Unless you are using a truly neutral color (like beige, cream or white), pick your paint color based on the furniture, artwork or bedding (if in a bedroom) that will be in the Sacred Soul Space. Keep in mind that different colors have different psychological and physiological emotions they evoke, as we've already covered, so choose color according to the type of room you are designing. If you are going to paint your room, do this before you add anything back into the room.

Accessories, particularly the soft surface accessories like rugs, curtains and pillows are an easy way to add in colors.

Colors I want to incorporate in my room include:

Add Furniture

Arrange the furniture so it is conducive to the optimal movement and energy patterns discussed in chapter four, while taking into account special features of the room.

Draw a rough schematic of your room, including windows and doors. With a pencil, draw how your furniture might fit within the room (roughly to scale). Draw a few different scenarios if your room is challenging. When in doubt, try it out (in person). Don't be afraid to try a few different placements of furniture in your space to find the configuration that feels the best and allows for the most energy to flow. Your furniture must be in place before you add other elements.

Hang Artwork

Add artwork to your walls. The placement of art will depend on furniture location and wall size. As a reminder, you want to make sure there is a good amount of space around each piece of art or collage of art on a wall so it doesn't feel too crowded. Unless there is a tall piece of furniture that you will be placing artwork above, hang artwork so that the midpoint is at roughly 5'6" (for the most comfortable look and feel). Before you hang any of the pieces, decide where each of them will go. Make sure they all fit where they need to and they look good together. Adjust as needed before you start hammering. If you have a vision board you want to include in the space, treat the board as a piece of artwork, so that it has its own special space on a wall.

Artwork I want to hang:

Add in Accessories

Now that artwork has been placed, accessories will complete the overall look of the design. If a table is small, use the triangulation method with three items maximum. Add in pillows, curtains and rugs. Are there any plants you want to bring into the space? Rearrange as needed until you like the look of what you have created.

PUTTING IT ALL
TOGETHER

Accessories I want to add:

_____

_____

_____

_____

_____

_____

_____

Add Final Touches

Crystals/Stones:

_____

_____

_____

Meaningful Imagery:

_____

_____

_____

Altar:

What is the location of the altar?

_____

What is the theme of the altar?

_____

Vision Board:

_____

_____

Essential Oils:

_____

_____

Sacred Soul Space I want to design:

Intention for Room

Identify your intention(s) for the room. What is the overall feeling you want to create? For example: calm, peaceful, relaxing, healing, inspiring, joyful, passionate, spiritual, trusting, secure, invigorating, etc. List the intentions below:

Colors for Room #3

Choose the colors you want to incorporate into the room to give you the feeling and intention you want to create. Your room can incorporate a few intentions, as long as they are compatible with each other rather than conflicting. For instance, if you are trying to create a peaceful, calming space, you might use blue and green, but you would not use red with those colors, unless it is in a very minimal way.

Determine how much of each color you might want and make a preliminary plan as to where and how you will use those colors (wall color vs. artwork, accessories or furniture).

For a big, bold look, use color on the walls in addition to the furnishings. For a subtle look, use a neutral color on the walls and bring in color with furnishings and accents. If you know you have very colorful art and accessories to use in the space, a neutral background can provide a nice backdrop to the main focal points in the room. Too much color can be chaotic and confusing and actually hide focal pieces.

All rooms will need a neutral color somewhere to ground everything for an optimal feel and look. This could be in the flooring, wall color or furniture.

Adding in color can be one of the most challenging design elements for you to do, but if you use your intuition, you will know how much of each color to incorporate. You might need to experiment and change things around to get the desired effect.

Paint is one of the easiest and least expensive ways to change the look of a room with a huge impact. Unless you are using a truly neutral color (like beige, cream or white), pick your paint color based on the furniture, artwork or bedding (if in a bedroom) that will be in the Sacred Soul Space. Keep in mind that different colors have different psychological and physiological emotions they evoke, as we've already covered, so choose color according to the type of room you are designing. If you are going to paint your room, do this before you add anything back into the room.

Accessories, particularly the soft surface accessories like rugs, curtains and pillows are an easy way to add in colors.

Colors I want to incorporate in my room include:

Add Furniture

Arrange the furniture so it is conducive to the optimal movement and energy patterns discussed in chapter four, while taking into account special features of the room.

Draw a rough schematic of your room, including windows and doors. With a pencil, draw how your furniture might fit within the room (roughly to scale). Draw a few different scenarios if your room is challenging. When in doubt, try it out (in person). Don't be afraid to try a few different placements of furniture in your space to find the configuration that feels the best and allows for the most energy to flow. Your furniture must be in place before you add other elements.

PUTTING IT ALL
TOGETHER

Hang Artwork

Add artwork to your walls. The placement of art will depend on furniture location and wall size. As a reminder, you want to make sure there is a good amount of space around each piece of art or collage of art on a wall so it doesn't feel too crowded. Unless there is a tall piece of furniture that you will be placing artwork above, hang artwork so that the midpoint is at roughly 5'6" (for the most comfortable look and feel). Before you hang any of the pieces, decide where each of them will go. Make sure they all fit where they need to and they look good together. Adjust as needed before you start hammering. If you have a vision board you want to include in the space, treat the board as a piece of artwork, so that it has its own special space on a wall.

Artwork I want to hang:

_____

_____

_____

_____

_____

_____

Add in Accessories

Now that artwork has been placed, accessories will complete the overall look of the design. If a table is small, use the triangulation method with three items maximum. Add in pillows, curtains and rugs. Are there any plants you want to bring into the space? Rearrange as needed until you like the look of what you have created.

Accessories I want to add:

_____

_____

_____

_____

_____

_____

Add Final Touches

Crystals/Stones:

_____

_____

_____

Meaningful Imagery:

_____

_____

_____

Altar:

What is the location of the altar?

_____

What is the theme of the altar?

_____

Vision Board:

_____

_____

Essential Oils:

_____

_____

Conclusion

We are all impacted by our environmental surroundings, whether we are aware of it or not. Thank you for taking the time to learn about Sacred Soul Space Design. Use this manual as a reference to design intentional spaces that truly inspire and rejuvenate you.

I encourage you to be conscious in your design efforts and keep your clutter to a minimum. Once you have designed your Sacred Soul Space and are living in it, you will notice changes in your life for the better. You will feel healthier. You will be inspired. You will be more focused and intentional. You will experience joy.

I hope I have educated you and inspired you as you read through and did the exercises in this manual. It is my sincere desire that you are able to utilize the information and incorporate the concepts into your everyday living environments.

Happy designing!

Appendix 1:
Essential Oils & Their Properties

There are some books that go into great detail about what each of the major oils does to the emotions and how they act as healing agents. The list of oils below will give you a good overview and a starting place to figure out which oils you may want to incorporate into your space. I also encourage you to research for yourself.

Arborvitae – Oil of Divine Grace – calming; may help enhance spiritual awareness and meditation as well as spiritual communication during rituals and ceremonies; peaceful, surrender, grounded, trusting, relaxed, grace

Basil – Oil of Renewal - helps maintain an open mind and increases clarity of thought, brings strength to the heart and relaxation to the mind; energized, renewed, rejuvenated, rested, strengthened

Bergamot – Oil of Self-Acceptance - reduces physical stress and helps depression; may help to relieve anxiety, depression, stress and tension; uplifts and refreshes; self-acceptance, optimistic, confident, hopeful, lovable, good enough

Birch – Oil of Support - influences, elevates, opens and increases awareness in the sensory system (senses and sensations); supported, firm, resolute, strengthened, grounded, connected, receiving

Black Pepper – Oil of Unmasking - comforting and stimulating; emotional honesty, authentic, courageous, motivated, self-aware, integrity

Blue Tansy – Oil of Inspired Action - calming, good for anxiety; inspired, initiative, committed, responsive, energized, motivated, purposeful, responsible

Cardamom – Oil of Objectivity - uplifting, refreshing and invigorating; may help with clearing confusion; objective, self-control, respectful, tolerant, patient, mental sobriety

Cassia – Oil of Self-Assurance – gladness and courage; helps to overcome fear; courageous, self-assured, unashamed, confident, valued, authentic

Cedarwood – Oil of Community - calming, good for tension, use when doing yoga; emotionally connected, belonging, supported, social bonds, sociable, community oriented

Chamomile (Roman) – Oil of Spiritual Purpose - calming, relaxing; relieves depression, insomnia and stress; eliminates emotional charge of anxiety, irritability and nervousness; may be used to sooth and clear the mind, creating an atmosphere of peace and patience; purposeful, guided, peaceful, fulfilled, relaxed, spiritually connected

Cilantro – Oil of Releasing Control - good for anxiety and insomnia; cleansing, liberated, detached, untroubled

Cinnamon – Oil of Sexual Harmony – good for depression; body acceptance, attractive, accepted, healthy sexuality, intimate (diffuse with caution)

Clary Sage – Oil of Clarity & Vision - reduces depression, particularly Postpartum; helps with emotional stress and mood swings; spiritual clarity, intuitive, open-minded, imaginative, spiritually discerning

Clove – Oil of Boundaries – influences healing, improves memory as mental stimulant, creates a feeling of protection and courage; empowered, clear boundaries, protected, courageous, independent, capable, proactive, integrity (diffuse with caution)

Copaiba – Oil of Unveiling - good for anxiety, helps activate past life regression memories; worthy, self-aware, clarity, forgiven, redefinition of self, purposeful existence

Coriander – Oil of Integrity - gentle stimulant for low physical energy, helps relaxation during times of stress, irritability and nervousness; may also provide calming influence to those suffering from shock or fear; true to self, inner guidance, integrity, unique

Cumin – Oil of Balanced Ambition – eases anxiety; balanced zeal, considerate, respectful, non-attachment to success, abundant thinking

Cypress – Oil of Motion & Flow - influences and strengthens and helps ease the feeling of loss; creates a feeling of security and grounding; flexible, trusting, flowing with life, adaptable

Dill – Oil of Learning - calms the autonomic nervous system; when combined with chamomile, can help fidgety children; engaged, motivated, integration, mental clarity

Douglas Fir – Oil of Generational Wisdom - helps to focus, creates a feeling of grounding and anchoring, can help balance the emotions and stimulate the mind while at the same time relaxing the body; generational healing, respect for elders, wisdom, learning from the past

Eucalyptus – Oil of Wellness - helps heal many symptoms and illnesses; able to heal; liberated, responsible, encouraged

Fennel – Oil of Responsibility - increases and influences longevity; courage and purification; responsible, in tune with body, satiated

Frankincense – Oil of Truth - helps focus energy, minimize distractions and improve concentration; eases hyperactivity, impatience, irritability and restlessness; enhances spiritual awareness and meditation; enlightened, loved, protected, wisdom, discerning, spiritually open, connected to father

Geranium – Oil of Love & Trust - helps release negative memories, taking one back to peaceful, joyful moments; helps ease nervous tension and stress, balances the emotions, lifts the spirit, and fosters peace, well-being and hope; emotional healing, empathetic, trusting, forgiving, gentle, loving, tolerant, open

Ginger – Oil of Empowerment - influences physical energy, love, money and courage; empowered, committed, capable, purposeful, accountable

Grapefruit – Oil of Honoring the Body - helps to suppress the appetite, so you won't overeat; aids in weight loss, helps with depression and fatigue; balancing and uplifting to the mind, helps relieve anxiety; respectful of physical needs, body acceptance, nourished, healthy relationship with food

Helichrysum – Oil for Pain - uplifting to the subconscious, calms feelings of anger; healing, courageous, hopeful, transforming, persevering, determined

Jasmine – Oil of Sexual Purity & Balance - very uplifting to the emotions; increases intuitive powers and wisdom; promotes powerful, inspirational relationships; produces a feeling of confidence, energy, euphoria and optimism; reduces anxiety, apathy, depression, indifference and listlessness; healthy sexuality, pure intentions, innocent, healing, self-acceptance, intimate, trust, safe

Juniper Berry – Oil of the Night - evokes feelings of health, love and peace; helps to elevate one's spiritual awareness; protected, peaceful dreaming, courageous, self-aware

Kumquat – Oil of Authentic Presence – unstudied, authentic, real, honest, sincere, unpretentious, aligned

Lavender – Oil of Communication & Calm - promotes consciousness, health, love, peace and a general sense of well-being; nurtures creativity, helps concentration and depression, relieves grief/sorrow, physical stress, helps relaxation, relieves stress and tension, aids sleep; open communication, calm, expressive, emotional honesty, self-aware, peace of mind

Lemon – Oil of Focus - promotes health, healing, physical energy and purification; soothes anxiety, helps with concentration, eases depression as well as grief and sorrow; helps relaxation and removes stress; uplifting, invigorating, enhancing and warming; focused, energized, mental clarity, alert, rational, joyful

Lemongrass – Oil of Cleansing - promotes awareness and purification; spiritual clarity, cleansing, nonattachment, simplicity, discerning, releasing what is no longer needed

Lime – Oil of Zest for Life - stimulating and refreshing, helps overcome exhaustion, depression, and listlessness; helps memory and nervousness; promotes a sense of well-being; courageous, emotionally honest, engaged, revitalized, determined, grateful for life

Litsea – Oil of Manifestation – inspired, intuitive, aligned, receptive, manifesting, trust of inner voice, clarity, open to possibilities

Manuka – Oil of Being Upheld – soothed, comforted, healing, loved, cared for, upheld, known by the Divine, grateful, transcendence, safe and shielded

Marjoram – Oil of Connection - eases physical stress, promotes peace and sleep, may help with seeing the future in dreams; emotionally open and connected, close relationships, softhearted, loving, ability to trust

Melaleuca (Tea tree) – Oil of Energetic Boundaries - promotes cleansing and purity; energetic boundaries, healthy and respectful connections, empowered, resilient, safe

Melissa – Oil of Light - calming and uplifting to balance emotions, supports body and mind; enlightened, joyful, energized, integrity, spiritually connected, contagious enthusiasm, liberated, optimistic

Myrrh – Oil of Mother Earth - promotes awareness, uplifting; safe in the world, healthy attachments, trusting, bonding, maternal connection, nurtured, loved, secure, grounded

Neroli (Orange Blossom) – Oil of Shared Purpose & Partnership - helps with anxiety and stress, relaxing; patient, empathetic, kind, tolerant, fidelity, calm, intimate, sexual desire, resilient, cooperative, committed

Orange (Wild Orange) – Oil of Abundance - helps with anxiety, calming, uplifting, brings in abundance; abundant, sense of humor, playful, generous, spontaneous, creative, joyful

Oregano – Oil of Humility & Nonattachment - strengthens feelings of security; humble, nonattachment, willing, teachable, flexible

Patchouli – Oil of Physicality - sedating, calming and relaxing, reduces anxiety, influences sex, physical energy and money; grounded, confident, moderation, body connection and acceptance, balanced, stable, physically expressive

Peppermint – Oil of a Buoyant Heart - purifying and stimulating to conscious mind, aids in memory and mental performance; helps alertness, gives energy, reduces anger; buoyant, optimistic, relieved, strength to face emotional pain

Petitgrain – Oil of Ancestry - uplifting and refreshing, helps to refresh the senses, clears confusion, reduces mental fatigue and reduces depression, stimulates the mind, supports memory and brings joy to the heart; pioneering, chain-breaking, cultivating healthy traditions, embracing positive family connections

Red Mandarin – Oil of Childlike Perspective – seeing sweetness in life, wonder in parenting, refreshed, joy in simple moments, cherishing childhood, innocent, positive perspective

Rose – Oil of Divine Love - stimulating and elevating to the mind, creating a sense of well-being; loved, compassionate, healing, tenderhearted, accepted, empathy, receiving divine love

Rosemary – Oil of Knowledge & Transition - stimulates memory, opens the conscious mind; mental clarity, knowledgeable, teachable, enlightened, open to new experiences, ability to adjust

Sandalwood – Oil of Sacred Devotion - calms, harmonizes and balances the emotions; enhances meditation, good for yoga; humble, spiritual devotion, spiritual clarity, still, surrender, connected to higher consciousness

Siberian Fir – Oil of Aging & Perspective - emotional balance, energizing, eases fatigue, relaxing; comforted, forgiveness, perspective, honest, wisdom, living in the present, optimistic, adaptable, peaceful

Spearmint – Oil of Confident Speech - helps open and release emotional blocks to bring about feelings of balance, acts as an antidepressant, uplifting; confident, articulate communication, clarity, courageous

Spikenard – Oil of Gratitude - calms nerves, balancing, soothing and harmonizing, helps with insomnia and stress; grateful, acceptance, content, peaceful

Tangerine – Oil of Cheer & Creativity - sedating and calming to nervous system; when paired with marjoram, it soothes emotions of grief, anger and shock; cheerful, fun, creative, spontaneous, fulfilled, lighthearted, joyful, optimistic

Thyme – Oil of Releasing & Forgiving - helps energize in times of physical weakness and stress; aids concentration; uplifting and helps relieve depression; forgiving, tolerant, patient, openhearted, understanding, emotional release

Vetiver – Oil of Centering & Descent - helps focus and concentration, relieves stress and helps people recover from emotional traumas and shock; helps induce a restful sleep; centered, grounded, present, emotionally aware and connected

White Fir – Oil of Generational Healing - creates a feeling of grounding, anchoring and empowerment, stimulates the mind while allowing the body to relax, creates the symbolic effect of an umbrella protecting the earth and bringing energy in from the universe; generational healing, healthy patterns, healthy connections, forging new pathways, spiritual protection

Wintergreen – Oil of Surrender - influences, elevates, opens and increases awareness in sensory systems; surrender, relying on divine grace, nonattachment, teachable, strengthened

Ylang Ylang – Oil of the Inner Child - influences sexual energy and enhances relationships, calming, relaxing, stress-relieving, tension-relieving, alleviates anger; playful, free, intuitive, emotionally connected, healing, joyful, innocent

Appendix 2:
Stones/Crystals

Stones/Crystals by Color

Red Stones: Cinnabar, Coral, Garnet, Jasper, Ruby, Tourmaline

Orange Stones: Agate, Calcite, Carnelian, Creedite, Quartz, Salt Lamp, Selenite, Soapstone

Yellow Stones: Amber, Chrysoprase, Citrine, Danburite, Desert Rose, Diamond, Garnet, Golden Healer Lemurians, Honey Dogtooth Calcite, Jasper, Kunzite, Moonstone, Onyx, Pyrite, Sapphire, Soapstone, Tiger's Eye, Topaz, Tourmaline

Green Stones: Agate, Apatite, Apophyllite, Aquamarine, Aventurine, Chrysoprase, Dioptase, Emerald, Fluorite, Green Kyanite, Halite, Jade, Jasper, Kunzite, Malachite, Moldavite, Onyx, Peridot, Prehnite, Quartz, Sapphire, Serpentine, Soapstone, Tourmaline, Turquoise

Teal/Turquoise Stones: Amazonite, Aquamarine, Chrysocolla, Opal, Selenite, Turquoise

Blue Stones: Agate, Amazonite, Angelite, Aqua Aura, Aquamarine, Azurite, Quartz, Calcite, Celestine, Chrysocolla, Diamond, Jasper, Kyanite, Lapis Lazuli, Larimar, Moonstone, Onyx, Sapphire, Sodalite, Topaz, Tourmaline, Turquoise

Purple Stones: Amethyst, Ametrine, Charoite, Jasper, Kunzite, Lepidolite, Sapphire, Sugilite

Magenta Stones: Cobalto Calcite, Garnet, Ruby, Ruby Fuschite, Sugilite, Watermelon Tourmaline

Pink Stones: Calcite, Coral, Danburite, Diamond, Garnet, Halite, Kunzite, Lithium Quartz, Moonstone, Pink Tourmaline, Rhodochrosite, Rhodonite, Rose Quartz, Ruby, Ruby Fuschite, Salt Lamp, Sugilite, Topaz

White Stones: Agate, Apophyllite, Calcite, Coral, Danburite, Desert Rose, Diamond, Faden Quartz, Herkimer Diamond, Howlite, Lemurian Quartz, Moonstone, Opal, Pearl, Quartz, Selenite, Topaz

Gray Stones: Agate, Calcite, Howlite, Pearl, Smokey Quartz

Black Stones: Black Tourmaline, Chrysanthemum Stone, Garnet, Hematite, Obsidian, Onyx, Sapphire

Brown Stones: Agate, Amber, Calcite, Desert Rose, Garnet, Jasper, Quartz, Selenite, Soapstone, Tiger's Eye

Gold Stones: Citrine, Golden Healer Lemurians, Honey Dogtooth Calcite, Pyrite, Tiger's Eye, Topaz

Silver Stones: Hematite, Pearl

Stones/Crystals by Alphabet

The following is a list of some of the most common crystals with their meanings and the colors you can find them in. You can use this as a general reference. A good book to read for more in-depth information on crystals is *Crystal Therapy* by Doreen Virtue and Judith Lukomski. There is a plethora of information on the Internet as well.

Agate – awakens your inherent talents; transforms negativity and balances physical and emotional aspects of your being
Color: comes in different color varieties ranging from blue, green, red, orange, brown, white and gray

Amazonite – connects to inner power, intuitive wisdom, and universal love; boosts self-love; boosts metabolism; restores one's faith in life; encourages one to spread wings and fly
Color: pale blue-green

Amber – can help you obtain your goals when used with focused attention
Color: translucent brown and yellow

Amethyst – opens your third eye for meditation; develops intuition; enhances creativity and connects you with the divine
Color: lavender to deep purple

Ametrine – this is a mixture of amethyst and citrine, so it helps to open the third eye as well as to sharpen mental focus; great for meditation, peace, tranquility; releases negativity; corrects RNA/DNA in spiritual and physical bodies; helps you achieve dreams
Color: purple and yellow/gold

Angelite – used to develop clear communication with angelic realm, brings peace to the world, connects you with your angels and guides and used in psychic healing, works to remove fears
Color: milky blue

Apatite – increases intellect, imagination and intuitive awareness; expands service and humanitarian pursuits; meditation/awareness tool; enhances energies of other crystals/stones; brings harmony and inner peace on all levels
Color: olive green

Apophyllite – opens third eye for mediation and psychic abilities; profoundly calms the heart; provokes conscious astral travel; purifies and clears energy and reawakens courage and life purpose
Color: clear, green, peach and white

Aquamarine – reduces stress and quiets the mind; soothes fears and increases sensitivity; sharpens the intellect and clears confusion; opens clairvoyance, serenity, joy and peace
Color: pale blue to sea-foam green

Aqua Aura – stimulates the spirit and elevates one's mood; brings serenity, peace, purification and rest, along with angelic communication, inter-dimensional access to your guides; great for channeling, removes negativity, and cleanses/clears/repairs the auric field
Color: iridescent blue

Aventurine – a mystical stone of prosperity, creativity, imagination, calm and happiness; heals heart pain and accelerates the balancing of yin and yang energy within you; helps with abundance and prosperity
Color: deep green

Azurite – the stone of heaven and spiritual wisdom, great for grounding your heart and mind; a tool for healers in balancing chakras
Color: deep blue, sometimes with some green

Black Tourmaline – powerful protection; excellent for grounding excess energy; purifies/deflects and transforms negative energy, transforms/removes negativity; dispels fears, obsessions, and neuroses bringing emotional stability
Color: black

Blue Lace Agate – calms, uplifts, dissolves fear and doubt
Color: pale blue with white striations

Blue Quartz – releases fear; brings courage and reduces stubbornness
Color: pale blue

Calcite – boosts energy to the physical, mental, emotional and spiritual bodies; helps with aura balancing
Color: comes in different colors including blue, cream, orange, green, honey, brown, pink and gray

Carnelian – grounds, balances, and heals relationships; manifests thoughts into the physical, protection
Color: deep orange

Celestine – brings calmness and harmony; transmutes pain into love and light; assists with achieving a higher level of consciousness and personal truth
Color: light blue

Charoite – enhances psychic awareness and abilities; helps to discover and heal hidden fears
Color: dark lavender to blue purple with black and white veins

Chrysanthemum Stone – expands compatibility and removes obstructions; helps you move toward goals
Color: grayish black with white imprints

Chrysocolla – healing of the heart and emotions; gives you great inner strength in hard times
Color: light blue to blue green

Chrysoprase – helps to heal personal problems and lift depression
Color: green and yellow

Cinnabar – assists in creating profitable business transactions and a sense of abundance
Color: red

Citrine – attracts wealth and good fortune; enhances mental focus and clarity; brings happiness and lightness; increases self-esteem
Color: yellow/gold mixed with clear quartz

Cobalto Calcite – heals emotions; fosters unconditional love, compassion and forgiveness; cultivates self-love, mends broken hearts, heals grief, speeds healing process; manifests abundance, reduces stress
Color: pink to crimson

Coral – eases emotional distress
Color: red, pink, and white

Creedite – deeply spiritual, gives immediate access to a clear meditative state by activating the third eye, crown and etheric chakras above the head, expansive awareness and cleansing euphoria, facilitator for accessing and understanding ancient knowledge
Color: orange

Danburite – unlocks barriers and blockages with joy; best to use in conjunction with other crystals
Color: clear, white, pink and yellow

Desert Rose – enhances feelings of well-being and understanding your own personal value in the universe
Color: brown, tan, white and soft yellow

Diamond – stone of clarity, communication and commitment; enhances prosperity, spirituality and love
Color: clear, blue, pink and yellow

Dioptase – helps cultivate life balance; creates harmony while working on goals
Color: deep emerald green

Emerald – stone of successful love, loyalty and bliss; strengthens memory and focus; increases inner knowing, truth and discernment; deepens spirituality and consciousness
Color: green

Faden Quartz – helps repair holes in aura and etheric body; facilitates better communication between people and enhances relationships
Color: clear with vertical threads

Fluorite – clears negative energy; cleanses and renews chakras and transmutes everyone and everything into light and love; helps to deepen awareness and spiritual growth; helps ground energy and improve focus
Color: green mixed at times with purple, yellow and teal/blue

Garnet – stimulates passion, creativity and intention
Color: red, yellow, green, brown, pink and black

Golden Healer Lemurians – good for all types of healing; connects one to the spiritual worlds; accesses Christ consciousness; activates the solar plexus to join our will with Divine will; aligns chakras and balances yin/yang energy
Color: gold

Goldstone – guards against negative energy; restores balance to the sacral chakra; bridges the gap between the physical world and the spirit realm; boosts your drive and confidence
Color: brown, blue or green with copper sparkles

Green Kyanite – brings peace and compassion, calms heart and mind, tranquility, tolerance
Color: green with sparkles

Halite – enhances good will; elevates mood; diminishes mood swings and negativity; stimulates initiative and independent thinking; allows you to access your inner wisdom to solve problems
Color: pale pink or green

Hematite – excellent for grounding; protection and memory enhancement; enhances optimism and courage
Color: metallic silver/black

Herkimer Diamond – brings unbridled spontaneity and joy; balances the mental, emotional and physical levels; clears/opens chakras; relieves tension; brings peace of mind, astral travel, and abundance
Color: clear

Honey Dogtooth Calcite – aligns and bridges one's physicality and spirituality allowing divine connection to one's highest self in the here and now; great for meditation, calming, stress reduction, peace, harmony, and inter-dimensional communication
Color: gold

Howlite – calming for the heart and mind; strengthens patience and tolerance; helps sleep imbalances; absorbs anger and rage from self and others; stress reducer
Color: milky white with gray lines

APPENDIX 2:

STONES/CRYSTALS

Jade – cultivates growth toward profound self-realization; brings healing, serenity and tranquility; balances and heals; brings compassion, wealth and wisdom; assists with past-life recall and ancient wisdom
Color: green, but can also have lavender, white, black, yellow, red, brown, and blue

Jasper – prevents exhaustion; offers protections; increases fertility; aligns all chakras; boost organizational skills
Color: red, brown, yellow, pink, green, blue, and purple

Kunzite – connects to infinite source of love; purification on all levels; enhances expression of self-love, unconditional love and romantic love; removes obstacles in one's path; dissolves negativity; clears and protect auric field; inspires openness
Color: pale pink, lavender, clear, yellow, and green

Kyanite – excellent for communication; clears fears of and obstructions to speaking your truth
Color: blue with white striations

Labradorite – assists in astral travel, dreamtime healing, and connecting to other dimensions and spirit guides; excellent for transformation on all levels; offers clarity
Color: iridescent metallic with deep green/blue/yellow

Lapis Lazuli – awakens you to the divine perfection you are; opens your third eye; shows you your true authentic self; enhances self-acceptance; releases depression
Color: deep cobalt blue

Larimar – helps release depression
Color: aqua blue with white intermixed

Lemurian Quartz – excellent for dream work and deep heart connections; inspires unconditional love for the Divine and each other; deepens connection to all humanity and circle of light protection; connects you to ancient information from past civilizations; aids in telepathy; promotes self-confidence
Color: clear with light-encoded horizontal lines

Lepidolite – great for stress reduction; allows one to transition out of difficult challenges in life; inspires childlike love and acceptance; strengthens discovery of Higher Self
Color: lavender to violet purple with sparkling specks

Lithium Quartz – brings emotional peace, stress release and relaxation; balances brain and emotions; moves anger and grief to the surface for healing; aids in sleeping and anxiety disorders; calming, soothing, and uplifting
Color: clear with pale pink

Malachite – deep spiritual, emotional and physical healing; brings strength and power, respect, and protection; absorbs negativity, clears electromagnetic fields, releases fears and depression; fosters transformation, change and risk taking; attracts abundance when working through heart's life purpose
Color: rich dark/light greens

Moldavite – elevates consciousness with awareness, connecting you to ascended Masters
Color: green

Moonstone – stone of new beginnings; assists in positive change and protects travelers
Color: creamy white, blue, pink, and yellow

Obsidian – protects sensitive people; rids negativity and pain
Color: black with some color variations within it including rainbow, green, mahogany, smoky, snow-flake white

Onyx – increases awareness of visions and dreams; increases concentration with self-control and grounding
Color: black, blue, green and yellow

Opal – balances all levels of an individual, creating harmony
Color: iridescent of rainbow colors; white, orange, black, blue, pink, teal and purple

Pearl – represents integrity, purity and grace, works well with other stones
Color: white/cream and grayish black

Peridot – helps create prosperity; clears heart chakra; helps to understand relationships
Color: olive and yellowish to darker green

Pink Tourmaline – inspires unconditional love and forgiveness of self and others, as well as grace, gentleness, compassion and kindness
Color: pale pink

Prehnite – strengthens life force energy and calms at the same time; eases worries and restlessness; aids spirit communication through meditation and visualization as well as astral travel; stimulates inner knowing and psychic power
Color: light to dark green

Pyrite (fool's gold) – creates abundance; increases meditative abilities
Color: yellowish-gold

Quartz – clears negative energy; magnifies intention from the highest good; great for meditation, spiritual manifestation, general healing, and spiritual development
Color: clear, blue, green, rose, smoky brown and orange

Rainbow Quartz – gives hope, promise, renewed life; brings pure joy and lightness of heart
Color: clear with rainbow inclusions

Rhodochrosite – helps create a balanced, loving approach to life; eases moments of change
Color: creamy pink and white

Rhodonite – expands heart chakra; opens one to unconditional love and increases service to mankind; inspires generosity of spirit, self-love; calms, eases anger; brings emotional balance and confidence; enhances passionate love; mends a broken heart; heals trauma and abuse
Color: pale pink with some black striations

Rose Quartz – healing crystal that enhances self-love, beloved purity of self and others, unconditional love; nurtures
Color: pink

Ruby – strengthens leadership, power, protection and detoxification; strengthens love
Color: deep red, pink, magenta

Ruby Fuchsite – balances physical health; brings peace to daily routines; releases stress; induces bliss
Color: pinkish red with pale green

Salt Lamp (Himalayan) – cleanses and purifies the air; provides a calming and relaxing atmosphere; great for healing; clears negative energy
Color: orange, pink and iron striations

Sapphire – quiets the mind, helps with organizational skills, and enhances intuition
Color: blue, yellow, green, black and purple

Selenite – increases insight for promoting justice during disputes; helps with angelic guidance; allows one to access past lives; removes energy blocks from physical and etheric bodies; brings mental flexibility needed to maintain loving relationships with ease; expands crown chakra
Color: milky clear, orange, red, brown and green blue

Serpentine – can clear all chakras simultaneously; stone of divine feminine
Color: variations of green with yellow and black flecks

Smokey Quartz – transforms negative energy; releases anger and resentment; offers protection; brings one to the present moment
Color: brown/grey

Soapstone – brings peace; assists with changes in life and gratitude
Color: earthy orange, brown, green and yellow

Sodalite – manifests your ability to find soul mate; fosters companionship; opens a heart to the impossible; enhances self-esteem and trust in others
Color: deep blue with white veins

Sugilite – removes physical and emotional pain and trauma; dispels negativity/anger; opens one to spiritual energy/growth; helps one discover soul's purpose; intense protection, psychic development, channeling; keeps soul safe
Color: pinkish-purple with a hint of black

Tiger's Eye – offers protection; brings good luck, mental clarity, willpower, purpose, courage and self-confidence
Color: gold to red with black bands

Topaz – brings information and healing at a faster rate for those with open hearts
Color: blue, pink, golden and clear

Tourmaline – commands energy on its own and when used with other stones creates a chakra bridge of spiritual expansion
Color: black, green, pink, watermelon, red, yellow and blue

Turquoise – heals the spirit; induces wisdom, trust, and kindness
Color: blue, green and turquoise with black veins or coloration

APPENDIX 2:

STONES/CRYSTALS

Bibliography

Andrews, Ted, *Animal Speak*. Minnesota: Llewellyn Publications. 1993.

Birren, Faber, *Color Psychology and Color Therapy: A Factual Study of the Influence of Color on Human Life*. Montana: Kessinger Publishing. 1961.

Chauran, Alexandra, *Clearing Clutter: Physical, Mental and Spiritual*. Minnesota: Llewellyn Publications. 2015.

Emotions & Essential Oils. Utah: Enlighten Alternative Healing, LLC, 2017.

Farmer, Dr. Steven, *Pocket Guide to Spirit Animals*. California: Hay House, Inc., 2012.

Giliam, James and David Unruh. "The Effects of Baker-Miller Pink on Biological, Physical and Cognitive Behaviour." *Journal of Orthomolecular Medicine* 3.4 (1988): 202-206.

Kwallek, Nancy, Kokyung Soon and Carol M. Lewis. "Work week productivity, visual complexity, and individual environmental sensitivity in three offices of different color interiors." *Color Research & Application* 32. 130 (2007) - 143. 10.1002/col.20298.

Linn, Denise, *Feng Shui For the Soul*. California: Hay House, Inc., 1999.

Linn, Denise, *Sacred Space*. New York: Random House Publishing Group, 1995.

Meyer, Regula, *Animal Messengers: An A-Z Guide to Signs and Omens in the Natural World*. Vermont: Bear & Company, 2002.

Modern Essentials. Utah: AromaTools™, 2016.

Mohagheghzadeh A., P. Faridi, M. Shams-Ardakani, and Y. Ghasemi. "Medicinal Smokes." *J Ethnopharmacol*. 108.2 (2006):161-84.

Tchi, Rodika, *The Healing Power of Smudging: Cleansing Rituals to Purify Your Home, Attract Positive Energy and Bring Peace into Your Life*. California: Ulysses Press, 2017.

Virtue, Doreen and Lukomski, Judith, *Crystal Therapy: How to Heal and Empower Your Life with Crystal Energy*. California: Hay House, Inc., 2005.

Whitbourne, Susan Krauss. "5 Reasons to Clear the Clutter Out of Your Life." *Psychology Today*, May 13, 2017.

Lisa Poundstone, PhD

Dr. Lisa Poundstone is a scientist, award-winning interior designer, and spiritual coach and teacher. She has integrated her life passions to create Sacred Soul Space Design.

Lisa earned a PhD in Organismal Biology and Anatomy from the University of Chicago and was a professor of Biology specializing in anatomy, physiology and evolution of animals.

After leaving academia, Lisa followed her passion for interior design and began her business, Design Smart. In her nearly ten years in the industry, she has worked with thousands of clients to design and stage their homes and offices.

Lisa trained with Denise Linn and became a certified Advanced Past Life Regression Coach. She started her second company, Mystic Manta Coaching, working with clients to help them release blockages and limitations, as well as access hidden talents and abilities. She has also been connecting clients with their deceased loves ones and spiritual messengers and guides.

Lisa currently resides in Olympia, Washington with the love of her life, Skip, her two children, Nohwa and Curran and their two cats, Chana and Bindi.

In her spare time, Lisa enjoys kayaking, jewelry making, dancing, walking, reading, watching movies and spending time with her close friends and family.

Opportunities to Learn More About
Sacred Soul Space Design

✤ **FREE blog and other gifts:**

Sign up to learn concepts in design and be inspired by the world around you.

✤ **Sacred Soul Space Design – Online Course:**

If you desire additional help, the information shared in this manual is covered in great detail with numerous visual examples and explanations to guide you in creating your Sacred Soul Space. You will gain a more in-depth understanding of how to apply the concepts in your home and office.

✤ **VIP Design Service:**

If you prefer a personal hands-on experience with Lisa directly, she can help you to design your Sacred Soul Space remotely or in person.

For more information, visit

www.SacredSoulDesign.com